Who is Your Covering?

OTHER BOOKS BY FRANK VIOLA

Volume 1: Rethinking the Wineskin:
The Practice of the New Testament Church

Volume 3: Pagan Christianity:
The Origins of Our Modern Church Practices

Volume 4: So You Want to Start a House Church?
First-Century Styled Church Planting For Today

Volume 5: From Nazareth to Patmos:
The Saga of the New Testament Church

Straight Talk to Elders

Knowing Christ Togther

The Untold Story of the New Testament Church

**Visit the Present Testimony Ministry Web Site for
Free Downloads and Ordering Information:**

www.ptmin.org

WHO IS YOUR COVERING?

*A Fresh Look at Leadership,
Authority & Accountability*

Frank Viola

WHO IS YOUR COVERING?
A FRESH LOOK AT LEADERSHIP, AUTHORITY,
AND ACCOUNTABILITY

Third Edition

Copyright © 2001 by Present Testimony Ministry

Published by
Present Testimony Ministry
ptmin@aol.com / www.ptmin.org

Printed in the United States of America

*To all Christians who are seeking to meet under
the sovereign Headship of Jesus Christ,
with the same simplicity and purity
that marked the first believers.*

CONTENTS

FOREWORD

Remember the children's story, *The Emperor's New Clothes*? In it, a child verbalized that which the adults already knew but were hesitant to admit. Frank Viola, in this revealing treatise on "church authority," is like the small boy who finally blurted out, "But the emperor has no clothes on!"

Most believers probably already suspect that all is not well in Zion. But they are slow to question the status quo. After all, who wants to get branded as a troublemaker? The appalling fact of the matter is that most systems of church polity are utterly without Scriptural clothing!

So exactly who has authority over whom in the church? Should a pastor or even a plurality of elders control a church? What is accountability all about? Do denominations afford protection from doctrinal error and moral failure? Do we need modern day apostles to tell us what to do? How does the spiritual gift of "ruling" fit into things?

When I was a career pastor, I struggled with these issues. Surprisingly, none of them were really dealt with during my time in seminary. Once in the ministry, I discovered that most of the pastors with whom I discussed these things had never really thought through them either.

It was a major paradigm shift for me just to go from believing that there should be a single pastor in every church to believing in a plurality of elders. As it turned out, that was just the tip of the iceberg—there is so much more to this issue of leadership that the number of elders becomes almost irrelevant.

Frank's exposé is both thorough and Biblical. Every relevant passage dealing with leadership and authority is considered. I promise that this book will enrich your understanding of authority in God's kingdom.

May our Lord be pleased to use the truth contained herein to free the legions of followers and leaders who are trapped in the bondage of hierarchical church systems. As Jesus said, *"the truth shall set you free."*

Steve Atkerson
Atlanta, Georgia

PREFACE TO THE FIRST EDITION

In my last book, *Rethinking the Wineskin: The Practice of the New Testament Church*, I set forth the fundamental principles that governed the early church. The book was favorably received. And it also influenced the birth of a number of first-century styled churches.

As expected, some of these fresh and budding assemblies have suffered opposition from leaders in the organized church. In particular, they have generated acute questions about ecclesiastical (church) authority. In fact, they have been asked the same questions religious leaders asked our Lord centuries ago:

"By what authority do you do these things, and who gave you this authority?" (Matt. 21:23)

Unfortunately, not much has been written to answer this question. Thus I felt burdened to tackle the matter here and now.

Some of this book's content overlaps with that found in *Wineskin*. But it makes more complete my treatment of the subjects of leadership and authority. There is also a wide range of new material that I have embarked upon that does not appear in the earlier book. So this work is really a companion to *Wineskin*.

To my mind, the chief value of the book lies here: It presents a fresh model for understanding leadership, authority, and accountability. This model is both unique and countercultural. But it is not theoretical. I have watched it work in many churches that have returned to NT (New Testament) principle for their corporate life.

My aim in writing is both practical and theological. It is constructive rather than controversial. Nevertheless, because what I have written is so radically different from traditional understanding, it will doubtlessly raise eyebrows—and even hostility.

Frank A. Viola
Brandon, Florida
January 1998

PREFACE TO THE THIRD EDITION

This new edition of *Who is Your Covering?* reads clearer and easier than the original.

Like my first book, *Rethinking the Wineskin*, this volume continues to be translated into many different languages. This being so, I felt the need to lower the reading level so as to give my message a broader audience.

Those of you who have read the original work will appreciate the ease in which this new edition reads. I trust you will also appreciate the new look it has. The type font has been enlarged and the cover-candy upgraded.

I would like to thank Mike Biggerstaff for his 11th-hour proofing work. Therefore, any typos found can be laid at Mike's feet.

Frank A. Viola
Brandon, Florida
January 2001

INTRODUCTION

"So who is your covering?"

This is the terse query raised by many modern Christians whenever they encounter those who meet outside the institutional church. But what is at the heart of this inquiry? And what Biblical basis undergirds it? These are the questions that will engage us in this book.

It is my contention that a great deal of confusion and subnormal Christian behavior is connected with a modern teaching known as "protective covering." This teaching holds that Christians are protected from doctrinal error and moral failure when they submit themselves to the authority of another believer or organization.

The painful experience of many has led me to conclude that the "covering" teaching is a matter that greatly troubles Zion today. And it desperately begs for critical reflection.

In the following pages, I attempt to cut through the fog that surrounds the difficult issues attached to the "covering" teaching. Thorny issues like church leadership, spiritual authority, discipleship, and accountability. I also seek to outline a comprehensive model for understanding how authority operates in the *ekklesia* (church).

Is "Covering" Covered in the Bible?

Strikingly, the word "covering" only appears once in the entire NT. It is used in connection with a woman's head covering (1 Cor. 11:15). While the Old Testament uses the word sparingly, it always uses it to refer to a piece of natural clothing. It never uses it in a spiritual way. Nor is it ever used in connection with authority and submission.

So the first thing we can say about "covering" is that there is scant Biblical evidence upon which to construct a doctrine! Yet despite this fact, countless Christians glibly parrot the "who-is-your-covering" question. Some even push it as a litmus test to measure the authenticity of a church or ministry.

If the Bible is silent with respect to "covering," what do people mean when they ask, "Who is your covering?" Most people (if pressed) would rephrase the question to be: "To what person are you accountable?"

But this raises another sticky point. The Bible *never* consigns accountability to human beings! It consigns it exclusively to God (Matt. 12:36; 18:23; Luke 16:2; Rom. 3:19; 14:12; 1 Cor. 4:5; Heb. 4:13; 13:17; 1 Pet. 4:5).

Consequently, the Biblically sound answer to the "to-whom-are-you-accountable?" question is simply: *"I am accountable to the same person you are—God!"* Strangely, however, this answer is usually a prescription for misunderstanding and a recipe for false accusation.

So while the timbre and key of "accountability" slightly differs from that of "covering," the song is essentially the same. And it is one that does not harmonize with the unmistakable singing of Scripture.

Unearthing the Real Question Behind Covering

Let us widen the question a bit. What do people *really* mean when they push the "covering" question? I submit that what they are really asking is: *"Who controls you?"*

Common (mis)teaching about "covering" really boils down to questions about who controls whom. And the modern institutional church is built upon such control. Of course, people rarely recognize that this is what is at the bottom of the issue. For it is typically well clothed with Biblical garments. In the minds of many Christians, "covering" is merely a protective mechanism.

But if we dissect the "covering" teaching, we will discover that it is rooted in a one-up/one-down, chain-of-command style of leadership. Within this leadership style, those in higher ecclesiastical positions have a tenacious hold on those under them. Oddly, it is through such top-down control that believers are said to be "protected" from error.

The concept goes something like this. Everyone must answer to someone else who is in a higher ecclesiastical position. In the garden-variety, post-war evangelical church, this translates into the "laymen" answering to the pastor. In turn, the pastor must answer to someone with more authority.

The pastor typically traces his accountability to a denominational headquarters, to another church (often called the "mother church"), or to an influential Christian worker. (The worker is perceived to have a higher rank in the ecclesiastical pyramid.)

So the "layman" is "covered" by the pastor. The pastor is "covered" by the denomination, the mother church, or the Christian worker. Because each is accountable to a higher ecclesiastical authority, each is protected ("covered") by that authority. So the thinking goes.

This "covering-accountability" template is applied to all spiritual relationships in the church. And each relationship is artificially cut to fit the template. No relationship can be had outside of it—especially that of "laymen" to "leaders."

But this line of reasoning generates the following questions: Who covers the mother church? Who covers the denominational headquarters? Who covers the Christian worker?

Some have offered the pat answer that *God* covers these "higher" authorities. But such a canned answer begs the question. For why is it that God cannot be the covering for the "laymen"—or even the pastor?

Hmmm . . .

Of course, the real problem with the "God-denomination-clergy-laity" model goes far beyond the incoherent, pretzel logic to which it leads. The chief problem is that it violates the spirit of the NT! For behind the pious rhetoric of "providing accountability" and "having a covering," there looms a system that is bereft of Biblical support and driven by a spirit of control.

CHAPTER 1

LEADERSHIP MODELS

If we strip it down to its bare roots, the idea of "covering" rests upon a top-heavy, hierarchical understanding of authority. This understanding is borrowed from the structures that belong to this world system. It in no way reflects the kingdom of God.

Let me unpack that a bit.

The hierarchical leadership structure, which characterizes the Western church, is derived from a *positional mindset*. This mindset casts authority in terms of slots to fill; objective job descriptions to carry out; titles to sport; and ranks to pull.

The positional mindset resonates with concern over explicit leadership structures. Terms like "pastor," "elder," "prophet," "bishop," etc. are titles representing ecclesiastical offices.

Parenthetically, an office is a sociological slot that a group defines. It has a reality apart from the person that fills it. It also has a reality apart from the actions the person in that office takes.

By contrast, the NT notion of leadership is rooted in a *functional mindset*. It portrays authority in terms of how things work organically. That is, how they function by God's life.

NT leadership places a high premium on the unique gifting, spiritual maturity, and sacrificial service of each member. It lays stress on functions, not offices. It emphasizes tasks rather than titles. Its main concern lies in activities like pastor-*ing*, elder-*ing*, prophesy-*ing*, oversee-*ing*, etc. To frame it another way, positional thinking is hung up on nouns. Functional thinking stresses verbs.

In the positional framework, the church is patterned after the military and managerial structures of our culture. In the functional framework, the church operates by life. Mutual ministry comes about naturally. Structure and rank are absent.

Native to positional/hierarchical oriented churches is a political machine that works behind the scenes. This machine promotes certain people to positions of ecclesiastical power.

Native to functionally oriented churches is the mutual responsibility and collegial interplay of the members. They listen to the Lord together and affirm each other in their Spirit-endowed gifts.

In a word, the NT orientation of leadership is organic and functional. By contrast, the positional/hierarchical orientation of leadership is fundamentally worldly. And there is a natural affinity between the positional/hierarchical orientation and the idea of "protective covering."

Jesus and the Gentile/Hierarchical Idea of Leadership

The ministry of Jesus on the subject of authority clarifies the underlying issues that lurk behind the "covering" teaching. Consider how our Lord contrasted the hierarchical leadership pattern of the Gentile world with leadership in the kingdom of God.

After James and John implored Him to grant them the glorified power-seats beside His throne, Jesus replied saying,

. . . You know that the rulers of the Gentiles LORD IT OVER THEM, and their great men EXERCISE AUTHORITY OVER THEM. IT IS NOT SO AMONG YOU, but whoever wishes to become great among you shall be your servant, and whoever wishes to be first among you shall be your slave; just as the Son of Man did not come to be served, but to serve, and to give His life a ransom for many. (Matt. 20:25-28, NASB)

And again,

. . . The kings of the Gentiles LORD IT OVER THEM; and those who HAVE AUTHORITY OVER THEM are called 'Benefactors.' BUT NOT SO WITH YOU, but let him who is the greatest among you become as the youngest, and the leader as the servant. (Luke 22:25-26, NASB)

The Greek word for "exercise authority" in Matthew is *katexousiazo. Katexousiazo* is a combination of two Greek words. *Kata,* which means down upon or over. And *exousiazo,* which means to exercise authority. The Lord also uses the Greek word *katakurieuo* in this passage, which means to "lord it over" others.

What Jesus is condemning in these passages is not oppressive *leaders* as such. Instead, He is condemning the hierarchical *form* of leadership that dominates the Gentile world!

That bears repeating.

Jesus was not just condemning tyrannical leaders. He was condemning the hierarchical form of leadership itself!

What is the hierarchical form of leadership? It is the leadership style that is rooted in the benighted idea that power and authority flow from the top down. Essentially, it is built on a chain-of-command social structure.

Hierarchical leadership is based on a worldly concept of power. This explains why it is endemic to all traditional bureaucracies. It is present in the vicious forms of liege-lord feudalism and master/slave relationships. It is also seen in the highly stylized spheres of military and corporate America.

While often bloodless, the hierarchical leadership style is undesirable for God's people. For it reduces human relationships into command-styled relationships. By that I mean relationships that are ordered along the lines of a military chain-of-command structure. Such relationships are foreign to NT thinking and practice.

Hierarchical leadership is employed everywhere in pagan culture. Regrettably, however, it has been adopted into most Christian churches today.

Summing up our Lord's teaching on this style of leadership, the following contrasts come into sharp focus:

◆ In the Gentile world, leaders operate on the basis of a political, chain-of-command social structure—a hierarchy. In the kingdom of God, leadership flows out of childlike meekness and sacrificial service.

◆ In the Gentile world, authority is based on position and rank. In the kingdom of God, authority is based on godly character. Note Christ's description of leaders: "let him *be* a servant," and "let him *be* as the younger." In our Lord's eyes, *being* precedes *doing*. And *doing* flows from *being*. Put differently, function follows character. Those who serve do so because they *are* servants.

◆ In the Gentile world, greatness is measured by prominence, external power, and political influence. In the kingdom of God, greatness is measured by inner humility and outward servitude.

♦ In the Gentile world, leaders exploit their positions to rule over others. In the kingdom of God, leaders deplore special reverence. They regard themselves "as the younger."

In brief, hierarchical leadership structures characterize the spirit of the Gentiles. Therefore, the implanting of these structures into the church is at odds with NT Christianity. Our Lord did not mince words in declaring His implicit disdain for the Gentile notion of leadership. For He plainly said: *"It is not so among you!"*

All in all, there is no room in Christ's teaching for the hierarchical leadership model that characterizes the modern church.

Jesus and the Jewish/Positional Model of Leadership

Our Lord also contrasted leadership in the kingdom with the leadership model that marks the religious world. In the following text, Jesus vividly expresses God's perspective on authority in contrast to the Jewish concept:

But do not be called Rabbi; for One is your Teacher, AND YOU ARE ALL BROTHERS. And DO NOT CALL ANYONE ON EARTH YOUR FATHER: for One is your Father, He who is in heaven. And DO NOT BE CALLED LEADERS; for One is your Leader, that is, Christ. But the greatest among you shall be your servant. And whoever exalts himself shall be humbled; and whoever humbles himself shall be exalted. (Matt. 23:8-12, NASB)

Gathering up the content of Christ's teaching here, we may glean the following:

♦ In the religious climate of the Jews there exists a class system made up of religious, guru-like specialists and non-specialists. In the kingdom, *all* are brethren in the same family.

♦ In the Jewish world, religious leaders are accorded with honorific titles. (Examples: Teacher, Father, Reverend, Pastor, Bishop, Priest, Minister, etc.) In the kingdom, there are no distinctions of protocol. Such titles obscure the unique honor of Jesus Christ and blur the NT revelation that envisions all Christians as ministers and priests.

♦ In the Jewish world, leaders are exalted into positions of prominence and glamorous display. In the kingdom, leaders find their work in the lowly towel of servitude and in the unassuming basin of humility.

♦ In the Jewish world, leadership is rooted in status, title, and position. In the kingdom, leadership is rooted in inward life and character. (In this vein, the current fad of bestowing honorary "doctorates" before the names of countless clergy is one example of how the modern church mirrors those leadership values that run contrary to God's kingdom.)

In sum, leadership according to Jesus is a far cry from what it is in most modern churches. Our Lord dealt a deathblow to both Gentile/hierarchical and Jewish/positional leadership models.

These ego-massaging models are incompatible with the primitive simplicity of the church and the upside-down kingdom of Jesus Christ. They impede the progress of God's people. They suppress the functionality of the believing priesthood. They rupture the image of the church as family. And they place severe limitations on the Headship of Christ. For these reasons "it is not so among" those who bear the name of the Savior!

The Apostles and Positional/Hierarchical Leadership

We have seen that our Lord condemned positional/hierarchical leadership structures. But what about Paul and the other apostles?

In contrast to popular thinking, the NT letters never cast church leaders in terms of "offices" and other conventions of human social organization. (We will deal with the various passages that some have used to support church "offices" later.)

Whenever the NT describes those *chiefly* responsible for spiritual oversight, it does so by mentioning the work they do. Hence, functional language dominates. Verbs are prominent.

Local overseers are called elders and overseers (Titus 1:5-7). This is simply because they elder-*ed*—they acted as seasoned models to the less mature (1 Pet. 5:3). They also over*saw*—they watched out for the spiritual well-being of the church (1 Pet. 5:2).

The task of the elders is also depicted by the metaphor of a "shepherd" (Acts 20:28; 1 Pet. 5:1-4). This is because they were caretakers. Just as literal shepherds care for literal sheep.

Consequently, equating overseers with a sociological slot (an office) can only be done at substantial risk. We have to evacuate "shepherd" of its intended meaning (one who tends sheep). We also have to evacuate "elder" from its intended meaning (an old man). Not to mention having to evacuate "overseer" from its native meaning (one who watches out for others).

It ought to be noted that all Christians participate in corporate leadership. Each member leads as he or she exercises his or her spiritual gift. As I have demonstrated in *Rethinking the Wineskin*, direction and decision-making come from the whole church. Oversight comes from the elders once they emerge (and this takes time).

The Role of the Elders/Overseers

In the Greek language, elder (*presbuteros*) merely means an old man. An elder, therefore, is a seasoned saint. A senior brother. That is its fundamental meaning.

NT elders were simply spiritually mature men—exemplary Christians who superintended (not controlled or directed) the affairs of the church.

Elders were not organizational figureheads. They were not hired pulpiteers, professional clergy, or ecclesiastical chairmen. They were simply older brothers (elders-in-fact) carrying out real functions (elder-*ing*, shepherd-*ing*, oversee-*ing*, etc.).

Their chief task was threefold: to *model* servanthood in the church; to *motivate* the saints for works of service; and to *mold* the spiritual development of the younger believers (1 Pet. 5:1-3). The elders were also the ones who dealt with sticky situations in the church (Acts 15:6ff).

But elders never made decisions for the church. As I have demonstrated in *Rethinking the Wineskin*, the NT method for decision-making was neither dictatorial nor democratic. It was consensual. And it involved all the brothers and sisters. As overseers, the elders *supervised* the work of others (instead of *substituting* for it). They prayed with their eyes open. They had their spiritual antennas perpetually raised to check for wolves. As older men, their wisdom was sought after in times of crises. When they spoke, their voices possessed the weight of experience.

Because they possessed a shepherd's heart, the elders bore the burdens of the church. They helped guide, protect, and feed the younger believers until they could stand on their own two feet.

Simply put, elders were spiritual facilitators who supplied guidance, provided nurture, and encouraged commitment in the church. Eldership, therefore, is something that one *does*. It is not a slot that one *fills*.

The NT bears this out rather clearly. For if Paul and the other apostles wanted to paint elders as officers, there were numerous Greek words they could have used to do so.

Significantly, however, the following Greek terms are missing from the apostles' ecclesiastical vocabulary:

- *arche* (a rank-and-file leader, head, or ruler)
- *time* (an officer or dignitary)
- *telos* (the inherent power of a ruler)
- *archisunagogos* (a synagogue official)
- *hazzan* (a public worship leader)
- *taxis* (a post, position, or rank)
- *hierateia* (a priest's office)
- *archon* (a ruler or chief)

The NT never uses any of these words to describe leadership in the church. Like that of Christ, the apostles' favorite word to portray church leaders is *diakonos*—which means a servant or a waiter.

The penchant to depict servant-leaders in the church as officers and professional clerics guts the true meaning of the Biblical language and cuts the nerve of the believing priesthood!

The Problem of the Modern Pastoral Role

By the same token, the commonly accepted notion of "sola pastora" (single pastor) is at odds with the NT. The Bible knows nothing of a person who stands at the helm of a local church, directs its affairs, preaches to it every Sunday, conducts its baptisms, and officiates its communion (or Lord's supper).

The highly specialized, professional "pastoral role" of modern Protestantism is a post-Biblical novelty that evokes a tradition of humane (but not so helpful) sacerdotalism! It is essentially a carry-over from Romanism (the priest). As such, it better reflects the weak and beggarly elements of the Levitical priesthood than anything found in the NT.

Just as serious, the pastoral role warps many who fill this position. Those who get seduced by the trappings of clerical professionalism are virtually always tainted by it. God never called anyone to bear the heavy burden of ministering to the needs of the church by himself.

Perhaps the most daunting feature of the modern pastoral role is that it keeps the people it claims to serve in spiritual infancy. Because the pastoral role usurps the believer's right to minister in a spiritual way, it ends up warping God's people. It keeps them weak and insecure.

Granted, many who fill this role do so for laudable reasons. And not a few of them sincerely want to see their fellow brethren take spiritual responsibility. (Many a pastor live with this frustration. But few have mapped the problem to their profession.)

Yet the modern office of "pastor" always disempowers and pacifies the believing priesthood. This is so regardless of how uncontrolling the person who fills this position may be.

Since the pastor carries the spiritual workload, the majority of the brethren become passive, lazy, self-seeking, and arrested in their spiritual growth. In this way, both pastors and congregations alike cannot help from being spiritually lamed by this unbiblical office.

While the NT calls Paul an "apostle," Philip an "evangelist," Manaen a "teacher," and Agabus a "prophet," it never identifies anyone as a pastor! In fact, the word "pastor" is used only once in the entire NT (see Eph. 4:11). And it is used as a descriptive *metaphor,* never as an ecclesiastical office. This flies in the face of common practice. Today "the pastor" is regarded as the figurehead of the church. His name is exclusively splashed on church marquees all across America. (One wonders why other ministries do not appear on these marquees when they are given far more attention in the NT.)

In the final analysis, the modern pastoral role undermines the Headship of Jesus Christ. It has a spiritually crippling effect on the church. It robs God's beloved priesthood (of *all* believers) of its full employment. Further, its mere presence diffuses and stalemates those "ordinary" believers who are equally gifted to shepherd and teach the flock. (Never mind that the Bible teaches that every church is to have multiple shepherds. Or that all members of the Body are to bear pastoral responsibility.)

Typically, if someone other than the pastor dares to shepherd or teach the sheep (even if he may be trustworthy, mature, and gifted), the pastor will feel threatened. He will then snuff it out under the guise of "protecting" the flock!

To be more specific and pointed, the present-day conception of "the pastor" is far removed from the thought of God. It puts the dynamic of NT community into an Old Testament straightjacket.

Yet regardless of the spiritual tragedies it engenders, the masses continue to rely upon, defend, and insist on the existence of this most unbiblical role. For this reason the so-called "laity" are just as responsible for the problem of clericalism as is the "clergy." As Jeremiah 5:31 says, *"the priests rule on their own authority; and my people love it so! But what will you do at the end of it?"*

If the truth be told, many Christians prefer the convenience of having someone other than themselves shoulder the responsibility for ministry and shepherding. In their minds, it is better to hire a religious specialist to tend to the needs of the brethren than to bother themselves with the self-emptying demands of servanthood and pastoral care.

The words of the old prophet capture the Lord's displeasure with this mindset: *"They have set up kings, but not by me: they have made princes, and I knew it not . . . "* *(Hos. 8:4a).*

In light of these sobering facts, one may intelligently ask how it is that the modern pastoral role remains to be the commonly accepted form of church leadership today. The answer lies deeply entrenched in the history of the Reformation. And it continues to be reinforced by current cultural imperatives.

In short, our 20th-century Western obsession with offices and titles has led us to superimpose our own ideas of church order onto the NT. Yet the very ethos of the NT militates against the idea of a single pastor system. It also militates against the idea of offici-elders. ("Offici" is shorthand for official.)

Scripture is equally at odds with the "*senior* pastor" concept. This is the common (but unscriptural) practice of elevating one of the elders to a prominent authoritative position. Nowhere does the NT sanction the notion of *primos inter pares*—"first among equals." At least not in any official or formal way.

This disconnect between "the pastor" and the other elders was an accident of church history. But because it meshes perfectly with our acculturated Christian mindset, modern believers have little trouble reading this false dichotomy into Scripture.

In sum, the modern pastoral role is little more than a one-size-fits-all blending of administration, psychology, and oratory that is packaged into one position for religious consumption. As such, the sociological role of pastor, as practiced in the West, has few points of contact with anything or anyone in the NT!

The Dramatic Lack of Attention Given to Leadership in the NT

Paul's letters make a lot of noise about exemplary action. But they show *no* interest in titular or official position. This fact deserves far more air-play than it has gotten.

Consider this. Every time Paul wrote to a church in crises, he always addressed *the church itself* rather than its leaders. This is consistent from Paul's first letter to his last. (Note that the "Pastoral Epistles"—1 Timothy, 2 Timothy, and Titus—were written to Paul's *apostolic* co-workers, not to churches.)

Let me repeat that. Every time Paul wrote a letter to a church, he addressed the *whole* church. He never wrote it to a leader or leaders!

Galatians 1:1-2: *Paul, an apostle . . . to the churches in Galatia.*

1 Thessalonians 1:1: *Paul, Silas and Timothy, to the church of the Thessalonians . . .*

2 Thessalonians 1:2: *Paul, Silas and Timothy, to the church of the Thessalonians in God our Father and the Lord Jesus Christ.*

1 Corinthians 1:1-2: *Paul, called to be an apostle of Christ Jesus by the will of God . . . to the church of God in Corinth, to those sanctified in Christ Jesus and called to be holy, together with all those everywhere who call on the name of our Lord Jesus Christ—their Lord and ours.*

2 Corinthians 1:1: *Paul, an apostle of Christ Jesus by the will of God, and Timothy our brother, to the church of God in Corinth, together with all the saints throughout Achaia.*

Romans 1:1,7: *Paul, a servant of Christ Jesus, called to be an apostle and set apart for the gospel of God . . . to all in Rome who are loved by God and called to be saints.*

Colossians 1:1: *Paul, an apostle of Christ Jesus by the will of God, and Timothy our brother, to the holy and faithful brothers in Christ at Colosse.*

Ephesians 1:1: *Paul, an apostle of Christ Jesus by the will of God, to the saints in Ephesus, the faithful in Christ Jesus.*

Philippians 1:1: *Paul and Timothy, servants of Christ Jesus, to all the saints in Christ Jesus at Philippi, together with the overseers and servants.*

More striking, every church that Paul wrote to was in a crisis (excepting the Ephesians). Yet Paul never appeals to the elders in any of them!

Take for instance Corinth, the most troubled church mentioned in the NT. Throughout the entire Corinthian correspondence, Paul never appeals to the elders. He never chastises them. He never commends obedience to them. In fact, he does not even mention them!

Instead, Paul appeals to the *whole church.* He shows that it is her responsibility to deal with her own (the church's) self-inflicted wounds. Paul charges and implores "the brethren" over thirty times in 1 Corinthians. He writes as if no officers exist. This is true for all of his other letters to churches in crisis.

If church officers did exist in Corinth, surely Paul would have addressed them to solve its woes. But he never does. At the end of the book, Paul tells the Corinthians to subject themselves to the self-giving Stephanas and his household. But he widens this group to others saying, "and to everyone who does likewise."

Notice that Paul's stress is on function, not on position. His stress is also placed upon the whole church. For the entire book of Corinthians is a plea to the entire assembly to handle its own problems.

Probably the most acute example of the absence of offici-elders in Corinth is found in 1 Corinthians 5. There Paul summons the whole church to discipline a fallen member by

handing him over to Satan (1 Cor. 5:1ff.). Paul's exhortation clearly runs against the grain of current thinking.
In today's thinking, only those possessing "ecclesiastical
clout" are regarded as qualified for such weighty tasks.

The difference in the way Paul thinks of elders and the
way most modern churches think of them could hardly be
more striking. Paul does not utter a whisper about elders in
any of his nine letters to the churches! This includes his
ultra-corrective treatise to the Galatians. Instead, Paul
persistently entreats "the brethren" to action.

In his last letter to a church, Paul finally mentions the
overseers in his opening greeting. But he does so in a very
fleeting way. And he greets the overseers only *after* he
greets the whole church (Phil. 1:1).

His letter opens with: "Paul and Timothy, bond-servants
of Christ Jesus, to all the saints in Christ Jesus in Philippi,
including the overseers and deacons" (NASB).This is a
rather strange order if Paul held to the notion of church
officers. Following this greeting, Paul talks to the church
about its present problems.

This trend is highlighted in the book of Hebrews.
Throughout the entire epistle the writer addresses the entire
church. Only at the very end of the letter does he off-
handedly ask the saints to greet their overseers (Heb.
13:24).

In sum, the deafening lack of attention that Paul gives to
elders demonstrates that he rejected the idea that certain
people in the church possessed formal rights over others. It
also underscores the fact that Paul did not believe in church
officers.

Peter's letters make similar music. Like Paul, Peter writes
his letters to the churches, and never to its leaders. He also
gives minimal air-time to elders. When he does, he warns

them against adopting the spirit of the Gentiles. He makes the specific point that the elders are *among* the flock, not lords *over* it (1 Peter 5:1-2).

The elders, says Peter, are not to "lord it over" (*katakurieuo*) the flock (1 Pet. 5:3). Interestingly, Peter uses the same word that Jesus used in His discussion on authority. His exact words were: " . . . the rulers of the Gentiles lord it over (*katakurieuo*) them . . . but it shall not be so among you" (Matt. 20:25).

This same emphasis is found in Acts. There Luke tells the story of how Paul exhorted the Ephesian elders to "be on guard for yourselves and for all the flock, *among* which the Holy Spirit has made you overseers . . . " (Acts 20:28, NASB). Notice that the elders are "among" and not "over" the flock.

James, John, and Jude write in the same strain. They address their letters to the churches and not to leadership. They all have very little to say about leadership. And they have nothing to say about official eldership.

It is quite clear, then. The NT consistently rejects the notion of ecclesiastical officers in the church. It also greatly downplays the role of elders.

Eldership vs. Brotherhood

It would do us well to ask why the NT gives so little air-play to the elders of the churches. The oft-ignored reason is surprising to institutional ears. It is simply this: The bulk of responsibility for pastoral care, teaching, and ministry in the *ekklesia* rests squarely upon the shoulders of *all* the brothers and sisters!

The richness of Paul's vision of the Body of Christ stems from his continual emphasis that *every member* is gifted, has

ministry, and is a "responsible believer" in the Body (Rom.
12:6; 1 Cor. 12:1ff.; Eph. 4:7; 1 Pet. 4:10). As a con-
sequence, ministerial responsibility is never to be closeted
among a few.

This explains why the word *adelphoi,* translated "brethren," appears 346 times in the NT. It appears 134 times in
Paul's epistles alone. In most places, this word is Paul's
shorthand way of referring to *all* the believers in the
church—both men and women. By contrast, the word
"elders" only appears five times in Paul's letters. "Overseers" only appears four times. And "pastors" only appears
once!

The stress of the NT, then, is upon *corporate* responsibility. It is the *believing community* that is called to
carry out pastoral functions. The brothers and the sisters
(=the whole church) are called to:

♦ organize their own affairs (1 Cor. 11:33-34; 14:39-40; 16:2-3)
♦ discipline fallen members (1 Cor. 5:3-5; 6:1-6)
♦ warn the unruly (1 Thess. 5:14)
♦ comfort the feeble (1 Thess. 5:14)
♦ support the weak (1 Thess. 5:21)
♦ abound in the work of the Lord (1 Cor. 15:58)
♦ admonish one another (Rom. 15:14)
♦ teach one another (Col. 3:16)
♦ prophesy one by one (1 Cor. 14:31)
♦ serve one another (Gal. 5:13)
♦ bear one another's burdens (Gal. 6:2)
♦ care for one another (1 Cor. 12:25)
♦ love one another (Rom. 13:8; 1 Thess. 4:9)
♦ be devoted to one another (Rom. 12:10)
♦ show kindness and compassion to one another (Eph. 4:32)
♦ edify one another (Rom. 14:19; 1 Thess. 5:11b)
♦ bear with one another (Eph. 4:2; Col. 3:13)
♦ exhort one another (Heb. 3:13; 10:25)

♦ incite one another to love and good works (Heb. 10:24)
♦ encourage one another (1 Thess. 5:11a)
♦ pray for one another (Jas. 5:16)
♦ offer hospitality to one another (1 Pet. 4:9)
♦ fellowship with one another (1 John 1:7);
♦ confess sins to one another (Jas. 5:16).

With dramatic clarity, all of these "one-another" exhortations incarnate the decisive reality that every member of the church is to bear the responsibility for pastoral care. Leadership is a corporate affair, not a solo one. It is to be shouldered by the entire Body.

Consequently, the idea that elders direct the affairs of the church, make decisions for the assembly, handle all of its problems, and supply all of its teaching is alien to Paul's thinking. Such an idea is fantasy and is bereft of Biblical support. It is no wonder that in elder-led churches spiritual maturity atrophies. And members grow passive and indolent.

Stated simply, the NT knows nothing of an elder-ruled, elder-governed, or elder-directed church! And it knows even less about a pastor-led church! The first-century church was in the hands of the brotherhood and the sisterhood. Plain and simple.

The example of the early church shows us how the ministry of the whole Body is to overshadow the oversight role of the elders. By virtue of their spiritual maturity, the elders simply *model* pastoral care to the rest (Acts 20:28-29; Gal. 6:1; 1 Pet. 5:1-4; Heb. 13:17b). Their goal, along with the extra-local workers, is to empower the saints to take responsibility for the flock (Eph. 4:11-12; 1 Thess. 5:12-13). Elders can simultaneously be prophets, teachers, and evangelists; but not all prophets, evangelists, and teachers are elders. (Again, the elders are the older, trusted men in the church.)

The emphasis of the NT, then, is upon the responsibility of the entire church. Leadership and pastoral responsibility fall upon the shoulders of *every* member. It does not fall on the back of one person or a select group.

In God's ecclesiology, *brotherhood* precedes *eldership*. Brotherhood supersedes eldership. And brotherhood over-shadows eldership. This explains why Paul's letters read awkwardly when we try to force an offici-styled vision onto them. Paul's understanding of leadership is corporate and it condemns overlordship. For this reason he speaks far more about the *brethren* than he does about elders.

In sum, the testimony of the NT denouncing position-al/hierarchical authority is unmistakably clear. And it is in direct harmony with the teaching of Jesus. As such, the final word to the Christian regarding Gentile and Jewish lead-ership structures is incarnated in our Lord's piercing phrase: *"But it shall not be so among you"* (Matt. 20:26). That is the linchpin of the whole matter!

CHAPTER 2

TRADITIONAL OBJECTIONS

For centuries, certain texts in the NT have been mishandled to support positional/hierarchical leadership structures in the church. Such mishandling has caused no small damage to the Body of Christ.

As we saw in our last chapter, the stress of NT ministry and leadership is on "doing" and "working" rather than on "office" and "position." In fact, there was no such thing as "church officers" in the early church.

The notion of positional/hierarchical authority is partly the result of mistranslations and misinterpretations of certain Biblical passages. These mistranslations and misinterpretations have been influenced by cultural biases. Such biases have cluttered the original meaning of the Biblical language. They have transformed simple words into heavily loaded ecclesiastical titles.

Yet these titles find no native soil in holy writ. Thus a fresh reading of the NT in its original language is necessary for properly understanding certain texts. For instance, a look at the original Greek yields the following sober insights:

♦ Bishops are simply guardians (*episkopoi*), not high-church officials.
♦ Pastors are caretakers (*poimen*), not professional pulpiteers.
♦ Ministers are busboys (*diakonos*), not clergymen.

♦ Elders are wise old men (*presbuteros*), not ecclesiastical officers.

Thankfully, a growing number of NT scholars are discovering that the "leadership" terminology of the NT possesses descriptive accents denoting special functions in the church rather than formal positions.

What follows is a list of common objections to the idea that leadership in the church is non-official, non-titular, and non-hierarchical. Each objection is followed by a clear response.

Objections From Acts and Paul's Epistles

(1) Do not Acts 1:20, Romans 11:13, 12:4, and 1 Timothy 3:1,10,13 speak of church officials?

The word "office" in all of these passages is a misnomer. It has no equivalent in the original Greek text. In fact, nowhere in the Greek NT do we find the equivalent of "office" used in connection with any ministry, function, or leader in the church. The Greek word for "office" is only used to refer to the Lord Jesus Christ in His High Priestly office (Heb. 5-7). It is also used to refer to the Levitical priesthood (Luke 1:8).

The KJV (King James Version) mistranslates Romans 11:13 to be " . . . I magnify mine office." But the Greek word translated "office" means service, not office. A better translation of Romans 11:13 is: " . . . I magnify my service (*diakonia*)."

Similarly, Romans 12:4 is better translated: " . . . all the members do not have the same function (*praxis*)." The Greek word *praxis* means a doing, a practice, or a function rather than an office or a position. The NIV (New International Version) and the NASB (New American Standard Bible) reflect this better translation.

Finally, 1 Timothy 3:1 says the following in the KJV: "If a man desires the office of a bishop . . . " But a more accurate translation puts it this way: "If anyone aspires to oversight . . . " (see J.N. Darby's translation of the Bible for this better rendering).

(2) Doesn't Paul's list of qualifications in the Pastoral Epistles, namely 1 Timothy 3:1-7 and Titus 1:7-9, indicate that elders are officers?

Paul's letters to Timothy and Titus were first dubbed the "Pastoral Epistles" as recent as the 18th century ("Pastoral Letters," *Dictionary of Paul and His Letters,* InterVarsity Press). But this is a misguided label.

Timothy and Titus were not pastors! They were apostolic co-workers who were mostly on the move. They only occasionally spent a long period of time in a single place. (For instance, Paul sent Titus to Crete and Timothy to Ephesus to strengthen those churches and sort out resident problems.)

Because they were itinerant church planters, Paul never called Timothy or Titus pastors or elders. These men were part of Paul's apostolic circle—a circle that was noted for its traveling (Rom. 16:21; 1 Cor. 16:10; 2 Cor. 8:23; 1 Thess. 1:1; 2:6; 3:2; 2 Tim. 2:15; 4:10).

All that is written in 1 Timothy, 2 Timothy, and Titus must be understood from that standpoint. It certainly explains some of the differences between these epistles and the rest of Paul's letters. In Timothy and Titus, the Body metaphor is wholly absent. The "brethren" are only occasionally mentioned. And there is little emphasis on mutual ministry.

By the same token, we do not find anything resembling nascent Catholicism in these epistles. The Spirit of God as well as His gifts are mentioned. And leaders are understood to gain recognition by their example rather than by any held position.

What we have in these texts, then, are the essential *qualities* of a true overseer, not a list of *qualifications* for an office that can be ticked off with a pencil.

The summation of all these qualities are: spiritual character and faithfulness. Moral rectitude and responsibility. Godliness and stability. Paul's lists, therefore, merely served as guides to Timothy and Titus in helping them identify and affirm overseers in the churches they worked with (1 Tim. 5:22; Titus 1:5).

Further, the flavor of these texts in the Greek is one of function rather than officialdom. Paul himself does not call an overseer an office-bearer. He calls it a "noble task" (1 Tim. 3:1b, NIV). Moreover, functional language is also employed when Paul commends honor to those elders who "guide well" and who "labor" in teaching (1 Tim. 5:17).

Therefore, to conflate the overseers in these texts with modern ecclesiastical "officers"—like the modern pastor—is pure fantasy. It is purely a function of our tendency to bring our organizational conventions to the NT and read them back into it. It is the result of a learned cultural framework that we bring to the text and nothing more. In short, the language of function rather than office dominates the "Pastoral Epistles" just as it does Paul's other letters.

(3) 1 Corinthians 12:28 says, "And God has appointed in the church first apostles, second prophets, third teachers . . ." Doesn't this text envision a hierarchy of church officials?

This question is indicative of our penchant for reading Scripture with the tainted spectacles of human hierarchy. It is a peculiarly American foible to insist that every relationship be conceived in terms of a one-up/one-down hierarchal mode. Thus whenever we see an ordered list in the NT (like 1 Corinthians 12:28), we cannot seem to keep ourselves from connecting the dots of hierarchy.

Yet while we 20th-century Westerners like to think in terms of organizational flow charts, the Bible never does. It is an unwarranted assumption to think that every ordered list in Scripture is some sort of a veiled command hierarchy.

So to see hierarchy in Paul's catalog of gifts in 1 Corinthians 12:28 represents a culturally biased misreading of Paul. The question of authority structures is not being asked anywhere in this text. Therefore, we do not exegete hierarchy from it. We impose it upon it!

A more natural reading of this passage understands the ordering to reflect a logical priority rather than a hierarchical one. In other words, the order reflects *greater gifting* with respect to the building of the church (compare with 1 Cor. 12:7,31; 14:4,12,26). This interpretation meshes nicely with the immediate context in which it appears (1 Cor. 12-14).

Paul is saying that within the scope of church building, the apostle's ministry is the most fundamental. This is because apostles give birth to the church and sustain it during its prenatal development. Apostles break the ground and plant the seed of the *ekklesia*. (And that seed is Christ.)

Since apostles lay the foundation of the church, they are also ranked first (chronologically) in the work of church building (Rom. 15:19-20; 1 Cor. 3:10; Eph. 2:20). Interestingly, while apostles are placed *first* in the church building scheme, they rank *last* in the eyes of the world—Matt. 20:16; 1 Cor. 4:9!

Prophets appear second in Paul's list. This indicates that they immediately follow apostles in their value to church building. Much confusion (and abuse) surrounds the function of the prophet.

Briefly, prophets supply the church with vision. They give spiritual encouragement. Like the apostles, prophets unfold the mystery of God's purpose for the present and future (Acts. 15:32; Eph. 3:4-5). They also root out the weeds so the church can grow unhindered.

Teachers are mentioned third. They follow the prophets in their gift-value to church building. Teachers put the church on solid doctrinal ground. They supply instruction concerning God's ways. They also shepherd the saints through hard times.

To continue the metaphor, the teacher waters the seed and fertilizes the soil so the church can flourish and blossom. If we examine the teacher with an eye for chronology, teachers build the superstructure of the church *after* the apostles have established the ground floor.

This interpretation of 1 Corinthians 12:28 follows the path of Paul's thought far better than that of a hierarchical command structure where apostles "pull rank" on prophets—and prophets do the same with teachers. It also brings to the fore an important spiritual principle. That is, the absence of hierarchical authority does not mean egalitarian gifting!

While the NT affirms that all are gifted and have ministry, it equally demonstrates that God disperses His gifts in a diverse way (1 Cor. 12:4-6). Every gift is valuable to the Body of Christ. But some gifts are greater than others within their respected spheres (Matt. 25:14-15; 1 Cor. 12:22-24,31; 14:5).

This does not mean that those with greater gifts are greater in authority (or intrinsic worth) in some formal sense. But God has called each of us to a different work. And some have greater gifts for different tasks.

For instance, some are called to the work of church planting. Others are called to local evangelism. Still others are gifted to show mercy. All have different gifts with different responsibilities. Some bear a greater responsibility than others (Rom. 12:6; Eph. 4:7).

Within the sphere of our gifts, each member is indispensable to the general upbuilding of the church—even those members whose gifts are not outwardly impressive (1 Cor. 12:22-25). Therefore, every Christian in the Lord's house is responsible for using and increasing his or her gifts. And we are all warned against hiding them in the napkin of fear (Matt. 25:25).

In short, the idea that 1 Corinthians 12:28 denotes some sort of church hierarchy lacks argumentative force. The text has in mind greater gifting with a subtext of the chronological order of church building. It does not indicate a pecking order of an ecclesiastical hierarchy or an authoritative ladder for Christians to climb!

(4) Do not Acts 20:28, 1 Timothy 5:17, 1 Thessalonians 5:12, and Hebrews 13:7,17,24 say that the elders have "the rule over" the church?

The words "rule" and "over" in these texts constitute a poor fit with the rest of the NT. There is no analog for them in the Greek text. This is yet another case where certain translations have confused the modern reader by employing culturally conditioned religious terminology.

Let us deal with each passage stated in the above objection. The word "rule" in Hebrews 13:7,17,24 is translated from the Greek word *hegeomai*. It simply means to
guide or go before. In his translation of Hebrews, NT
scholar F.F. Bruce translates *hegeomai* into "guides" (*The
Epistle to the Hebrews*, NICNT, Eerdmans). These texts
carry the thought of "those that guide you" rather than
"those who rule over you."

Similarly, in 1 Thessalonians 5:12, the word "over" is
translated from the Greek word *proistemi*. It carries the idea
of standing in front of, superintending, guarding, and
providing care for. NT scholars like F.F. Bruce and Robert
Banks explain that this term does not carry the technical
force of an official designation. For it is used in the par-
ticiple rather than the noun form. It is also positioned as the
second in the midst of two other non-official participles
(F.F. Bruce, *1 & 2 Thessalonians*, WBC, Word; Robert
Banks, *Paul's Idea of Community*, Hendrickson).

Bruce translates 1 Thessalonians 5:12-13 as follows:
"Now we ask you brothers to know those who work hard
among you and care for you in the Lord and instruct you,
and esteem them very highly in love because of their work."
The same word (*proistemi*) appears in 1 Timothy 5:17. It too
is incorrectly translated "rule" in the KJV and NASB. In
addition, in Acts 20:28, the Greek text says that the elders
are *"en"* (among) the flock rather than "over" them (as the
KJV puts it).

In a similar vein, Paul's statement that overseers must
"rule (*proistemi*) their own houses well" in 1 Timothy 3:4-5
does not point to their ability to wield power. It rather points
to their capacity to bear responsibility for the supervision
and nurture of others. The home is where one's character is

tested the most severely. This is why Paul makes reference to it in his character sketch of overseers.

In all of these passages, the basic thought is that of watching rather than bossing. Superintending rather than dominating. Facilitating rather than dictating. Guiding rather than ruling.

The Greek text conveys an image of one who stands within the flock, guarding and caring for it (as a leading-servant would). It is reminiscent of a shepherd who looks out for the sheep. Not one who drives them from behind or rules them from above!

Again, the drift of apostolic teaching consistently demonstrates that God's idea of church leadership is at odds with those conventional leadership roles that are based on top-heavy rule.

(5) Doesn't Romans 12:8 teach that God gifts some believers to rule in the church? For Paul says "he that ruleth, [should do so] with diligence."

The KJV uses the word "ruleth" in this text. But the Greek word that appears here is *proistemi*. This word envisions one who superintends and gives aid to others. It does not refer to one who governs or controls them.

The text is better translated: " . . . he that guards and gives care, do so with diligence." Paul's thought here is clearly one of earnest oversight rather than dictatorial rulership.

(6) Do not Acts 14:23 and Titus 1:5 teach that elders are ordained, implying that they are church officers?

The mention of apostolic recognition (appointment) is at least as friendly to the functional mindset as it is to the positional interpretation. In Titus 1:5, the word translated "ordain" in the Greek is *kathistemi*. It means "to set."

In Acts 14:23, the word is *kirotoneo*. It means "to stretch forth the hand." Both terms carry the idea of acknowledging those whom others have already endorsed. This is how these words are used outside the NT in first-century literature.

Second, there is not a shred of textual evidence to support the idea that Biblical recognition bestows or confers authority. Paul never vested certain ones with authority over the remaining members of the community. The Holy Spirit makes overseers (Acts 20:28). Elders exist in the church *before* they are outwardly recognized.

Apostolic recognition merely makes public that which the Spirit has already accomplished. The laying on of hands is a token of fellowship, oneness, and affirmation. It is not one of special grace or transferred authority. It is a profound error, therefore, to confuse Biblical recognition with ecclesiastical ordination. The laying on of hands does not qualify religious specialists to do what lesser mortals cannot!

Instead, Biblical recognition is merely the outward confirmation by the church of those who have already been charged by the Spirit to a specific task. It serves as a visible testimony that publicly acknowledges those who "have the goods."

In modern house churches, public recognition constitutes a Trojan horse of sorts. Some men just cannot handle the recognition. It inflates their egos. The title gives them a power trip. Worse still, it transforms some into control freaks.

We must remember that in the first-century it was the itinerant workers who publicly acknowledged overseers (Acts 14:23; Titus 1:5). Therefore, it falls upon the extra-local workers to discern the timing and method of how overseers are acknowledged. (Modern house churches should read that sentence again!)

The recognition of overseers—when they emerge—should not be pressed into any rigid mold. Some church planters directly recognize overseers. Others do so tacitly. (In this regard, there is no Biblical backing for self-appointed or congregationally-appointed elders.)

The bottom line is that when we attach the recognition of elders to special ceremonies, licenses, seminary degrees, acclamation by vote, et al., we are speaking where the Bible does not speak.

We do well to keep in mind that in the NT, the principle of recognizing elders exists. But the method is open. It always has the sense of *recognizing* a dynamic function rather than *placing* into a static office.

Further, we are on safe Scriptural ground if elders are recognized by extra-local workers who know the church well. This safeguards the church from being controlled and manipulated by local, self-appointed leadership. To appoint elders in any other way is to drift outside Biblical bounds.

(7) Doesn't Paul use the word "apostle" as an official title when speaking about himself?

Contrary to common thinking, most of Paul's correspondence contains a subtext that affirms that he is *not* an offici-apostle. Granted, Paul regularly makes known his special function in the salutation of his letters. (A la "Paul, an apostle of Jesus Christ.") But he never once identifies himself as "the Apostle Paul."

This is a meaningful distinction. The former is a description of a special function based on Divine commission. The latter is an official title.

In fact, nowhere in the NT do we find any ministry or function in the Body deployed as a title before the names of God's servants. Christians who are "title-happy" need to reflect seriously on this!

(8) Doesn't Ephesians 4:11 envision a clergy? It says, "And he gave some apostles, and some prophets, and some evangelists, and some pastors and teachers . . . "
Not at all. Ephesians 4 has in view those gifts that equip the church for its diversity of service (vv. 12-16). The gifts listed in this text are actually gifted *persons* who empower the church (vv. 8,11). They are not the gifts which the Holy Spirit divides to each *individual* as He wills (1 Cor. 12:11).

Put another way, Ephesians 4 is not discussing gifts given to men and women. It is discussing gifted men and women who are given to the church. Apostles, prophets, evangelists, and pastors/teachers are people given by the ascended Lord to His church for its formation, coordination, and upbuilding.

Their chief task is to nurture the believing community into responsible roles. Their success is rooted in their ability to empower and mobilize the saints for the work of the ministry. In this way, the Ephesians 4 gifts equip (Greek: *katartismos* = mend or fit) the Body to fulfill God's eternal purpose.

These ascension gifts are not offices. Nor are they formal positions. The Greek has no definite article connected with these terms. They are merely brethren with peculiar "enabling" gifts designed to cultivate the ministries of their fellow brethren.

Apostles enable the church by giving it birth from the ground up. They also help it walk on its own two feet. (We will discuss the apostolic function in more detail in Chapter 5.)

Prophets enable the church by speaking to it the present word of the Lord. They confirm each member's gifting. They prepare the church for future trials.

Evangelists enable the church by modeling the preaching of the good news to the lost. Pastors/teachers enable the church by cultivating its spiritual life through the exposition of Scripture.

Parenthetically, some view pastors and teachers as separate ministries. Others see them as distinct dimensions of the same ministry. In the latter view, pastoring is the *private* side of this ministry while teaching is the *public* side.

The Ephesians 4 ministries (often coined "the five-fold ministry") are not the equivalent of church leaders. Apostles, prophets, evangelists, and pastors/teachers may or may not be elders.

In short, Ephesians 4:11 does not envision a hired clergy, a professional ministry, nor a special priestcraft. Neither are they a special class of Christians. Like Paul's catalog of gifts in 1 Corinthians 12:28, Ephesians 4 has in view special functions rather than formal positions.

(9) Doesn't the mention of "governments" in 1 Corinthians 12:28 show that the early church possessed church officials?

The Greek word translated "governments" in the KJV is *kubernesis*. According to NT scholar Gordon Fee, "the noun occurs three times in the LXX [the Greek Old Testament], where it carries the verbal idea of giving 'guidance' to someone" (*The First Epistle to the Corinthians*, NICNT, Eerdmans).

Fee says that this word is better translated "acts of guidance." It most likely refers to the act of giving wise counsel to the church rather than to individuals.

Therefore, to invest an official form of church polity into this word is unwarranted and untenable. The only "government" that the *ekklesia* knows is the undiluted government of Jesus Christ (Isa. 9:6)! While overseers supply supervision in the church, they do not "govern" or "rule" it. So the term "government" is a poor word to describe any spiritual gifting in the church.

(10) Doesn't the Bible say that Timothy was "ordained the first bishop of the church of Ephesus?" Doesn't it also say that Titus was "ordained the first bishop of the church of the Cretians?"

Some editions of the KJV have these notes annexed to the end of the so-called "Pastoral Epistles." But they do not appear in the Greek text. The translators of the KJV inserted them.

As we have already seen, both Timothy and Titus were not "bishops." Nor were they pastors. They were Paul's apostolic co-workers—church planters, if you will (Rom. 16:21; 1 Cor. 16:10; 2 Cor. 8:23; 1 Thess. 1:1; 2:6; 3:2; 2 Tim. 2:15; 4:10).

Significantly, the monarchical episcopate (the bishop system) developed long after the NT was completed. Thus the historical evidence that Timothy and Titus were "first bishops" is just as scanty as the idea that Peter was the "first bishop" of Rome! All of these suppositions conflict with the NT story. They are human inventions that have no basis in the Bible.

*(11) Acts 15:22 mentions "chief men among the brethren."
Doesn't this imply the existence of hierarchical authority in
the early church?*

The KJV translates this text using the terms "chief
men"—which gives it a hierarchical flavor. However, the
Greek word for "chief" is *hegeomai*. And it simply means
"leading" or "guiding." (Consult with the NASB and NIV.)
This text underscores the fact that Judas and Silas were
among the respected brothers in the Jerusalem church. They
were *responsible* men—probably elders. For this reason the
church of Jerusalem selected them as temporary messengers
to Antioch (compare with Prov. 10:26; 25:19). To exegete
hierarchy from this verse is untenable.

*(12) Doesn't Paul's metaphor of the Body of Christ dem-
onstrate that authority works in a hierarchical mode? That
is, when the Head signals to the hand, it must first signal to
the arm. So the hand must submit to the arm in order for it
to obey the Head.*

Anyone who is conversant with human anatomy knows
that the above description reflects a flawed understanding of
how the physical body works.

The brain sends *direct* signals to those body parts it seeks
to control through the peripheral nervous system. Consequently, the head controls all of the body's parts *immediately* and *directly*. It does not pass its impulses through
a chain-of-command schema invoking other body parts.

The head does not command the hand to tell the feet what
to do. Instead, the head is connected to the entire body. For
this reason the proper application of the body metaphor
preserves the unvarnished truth that there is only one
Authority in the church—Jesus Christ. All members are
under His immediate and direct control.

In this regard, the Bible is crystal clear in its teaching that Jesus Christ is the *only* mediator between God and man (1 Tim. 2:5). While the old economy had human mediators, the New Covenant knows no such thing. As participants of the New Covenant, we need no mediator to tell us to know the Lord. All who are under this covenant may know Him directly—"from the least of them to the greatest" (Heb. 8:6-11).

It is mutual subjection, not hierarchical submission, that engenders the proper coordination of the Body of Christ. (This subject will be dealt with more fully in a subsequent chapter.)

(13) Every physical body has a head. Therefore, every local body of believers needs a head. If it doesn't have one, it will be chaotic. Pastors are the heads of local churches. They are little heads under Christ's Headship.

This idea is born from the imagination of fallen man. There is not a shred of Biblical support for such an idea. It is pure fantasy! The Bible *never* refers to a human being as a "head" of a church. This title exclusively belongs to Jesus Christ. He is the *only* Head of each local assembly. Therefore, those who claim to be heads of churches supplant the executive Headship of Jesus Christ!

Objections From Other NT Documents

(1) Doesn't Hebrews 13:17 command us to obey and submit to our leaders, implying that church leaders possess official authority?

Again, a look at the Greek text proves useful here. The word translated "obey" in Hebrews 13:17 is not the garden-variety Greek word (*hupakouo*) that is usually employed in the NT for obedience. Rather, it is the word *peitho*. *Peitho* means to persuade or to win over. Because this word appears in the middle-passive form in Hebrews 13:17, the text ought to be translated: "Allow yourself to be persuaded by your leaders."

This is an exhortation to give weight to the instruction of workers (and possibly local overseers). It is not an exhortation to obey them mindlessly. It implies persuasive power to convince and to win over rather than to coerce, force, or brow-beat into submission. In the words of Greek scholar W.E. Vine, "the obedience suggested [in Hebrews 13:17] is not by submission to authority, but resulting from persuasion" (*Vine's Expository Dictionary of New Testament Words*, Macdonald).

Likewise, the verb translated "submit" in this passage is the word *hupeiko*. It carries the idea of yielding, retiring, or withdrawing, as in surrendering after battle. Those who occupy themselves with spiritual oversight do not demand submission. And we are to accord them with recognition.

We are also encouraged to be uncommonly biased toward what such people say. Not because of an external office they hold, but because of their godly character, spiritual maturity, and sacrificial service to the saints.

In the words of Hebrews 13:7, we are to "imitate their faith" as we "consider the outcome of their life." By doing so, we make their God-called task of spiritual oversight far easier to carry out (v. 17).

(2) The Bible teaches that those who watch over the souls of the church will have to give an account to God. Doesn't this mean that these people have authority over others?

Hebrews 13:17 says that those who provide oversight are accountable to God for this task. Because of their advanced maturity and spiritual gifting, God holds overseers responsible for caring for their fellow brethren. But there is nothing in this text that warrants that they have special authority over other Christians! (See the previous point.)

Being accountable to God is not the equivalent of having authority. *All* believers are accountable to God (Matt. 12:36; 18:23; Luke 16:2; Rom. 3:19; 14:12; Heb. 4:13; 13:17; 1 Pet. 4:5). But this does not mean that they have special authority over others.

(3) Didn't Jesus endorse official authority when He commanded His disciples to obey the scribes and Pharisees because they sat in "Moses' seat?"

Not at all. What Jesus said about the scribes and Pharisees was a rebuke to their practice of *assuming* instructional authority when they possessed none. Matthew 23:2 says, "The scribes and the Pharisees *have seated themselves* in the chair of Moses" (NASB).

Our Lord was merely exposing the fact that the scribes and Pharisees were self-appointed teachers. And they had usurped authority over the people (Matt. 23:5-7; Luke 20:46). His statement was an observation, not an endorsement.

The Lord made it unmistakably plain that despite their pretense before men, the scribes and Pharisees did not have any authority whatsoever (23:11-33). In fact, they taught the Law of Moses, but they did not obey it (vv. 3b, 23:23).

In this light, the verse that follows, which says "therefore *all* that they tell you, do and observe . . . " (NASB, v. 3a) cannot be understood as a blanket endorsement of Pharisaical authority. This interpretation utterly contradicts the next verse (v. 4). It also contradicts all those passages where we find Jesus resolutely breaking Pharisaical teaching—and commanding His disciples to do the same (Matt. 5:33-37; 12:1-4; 15:1-20; 16:6-12; 19:3-9, etc.)!

Instead, this phrase (in v. 3) must be interpreted by our Lord's reference to "Moses' seat." "Moses' seat" is a literal reference to a special chair set aside in each synagogue from which the Old Testament Scriptures were read (E.L. Sukenik, *Ancient Synagogues in Palestine and Greece*, British Academy).

Whenever the scribes and Pharisees were seated in "Moses' chair," they read straight out of Scripture. Because Scripture has authority, what they read from this seat was binding (regardless of the hypocrisy of the readers). This is the essence of Jesus' statement. The lesson is that even if a self-styled, hypocritical teacher reads from the Bible, what he says *from the Bible* has authority.

Therefore, to project an endorsement of offici-authority onto the lips of the Savior in Matthew 23:2-3 is an example of Jesus co-opted by Roman Papism! As such, it fails to keep pace with the historic context of the passage. And it reflects nothing of the Gospels themselves.

(4) Doesn't the Greek NT support the idea that the church includes clergy and laity?

The clergy/laity dichotomy is a tragic fault-line that runs throughout the entire history of Christendom. Yet despite the fact that multitudes have taken the high road of dogmatism to defend it, this dichotomy is without Biblical warrant.

The word "laity" is derived from the Greek word *laos*. It simply means "the people." *Laos* includes *all* Christians. The word appears three times in 1 Peter 2:9-10 where Peter refers to "the people (*laos*) of God." Never in the NT does it refer to only a portion of the assembly. It did not take on this meaning until the third century.

The term "clergy" finds its roots in the Greek word *kleros*. It means "a lot or an inheritance." The word is used in 1 Peter 5:3 where Peter instructs the elders against being "lords over God's heritage (*kleros*)." Strikingly, the word is never used to refer to church leaders. Like *laos*, it too refers to God's people. For they are His heritage.

According to the NT, then, all Christians are "clergy" (*kleros*) and all are "laity" (*laos*). We are the Lord's heritage and the Lord's people. To frame it another way, the NT does not dispose of clergy. It makes *all* believers clergy!

In sum, there is not a hint of the clergy/laity, minister/layman schema in the history, teaching, or vocabulary of the NT. This schema constitutes a false dichotomy. It is a religious artifact that stems from the post-Biblical disjunction of the secular and the spiritual.

In the secular/spiritual dichotomy, faith, prayer, and ministry are deemed the exclusive properties of an inner, sacrosanct world. A world that is detached from the whole fabric of life. But this disjunction is completely foreign to the NT ethos where all things are to bring glory to God. Even the stuff of our everyday lives (1 Cor. 10:31).

(5) Do not the seven angels of the seven churches in the book of Revelation validate the presence of a single pastor in a local church?

The first three chapters of Revelation constitute a flimsy basis on which to construct the doctrine of a "single pastor." First, the reference to the angels of these churches is cryptic. John does not give us any clues about their identity. Scholars are not sure what they symbolize. (Some believe they point to literal angels. Others believe they are human messengers.)

Second, there is no analog for the idea of a "solo pastor" anywhere in the NT. Nor is there any text that likens pastors unto angels.

Third, the idea that the seven angels refers to "the pastors" of the seven churches is in direct conflict with other NT texts. For instance, Acts 20:17 and 20:28 tell us that the church of Ephesus had multiple shepherds (pastors), not one. This is true for all first-century churches that had elders. They were always plural (see *Rethinking the Wineskin*).

Therefore, to hang the "sola pastora" doctrine on one obscure passage in Revelation is sloppy and careless exegesis. Again, there is no support for the modern pastor system in Revelation or in any other NT document.

Objections From the Old Testament

(1) In Exodus 18, Moses set up a hierarchy of rulers under him to help lead God's people. Isn't this a Biblical pattern for hierarchical leadership?

If we read this account carefully, we shall discover that it was Moses' *heathen* father-in-law, Jethro, who conceived this idea (Exod. 18:14-27). There is no Biblical evidence to suggest that God endorsed it. In fact, Jethro himself admitted that he was not sure if God would support it (Exod. 18:23).

Later in Israel's journeys, the Lord directed Moses to take a different course regarding the problem of oversight. He commanded him to commission elders to help bear the weight of responsibility. Significantly, Moses selected those men who were *already* elder-ing (Num. 11:16).

This strategy was organic and functional. In this way, it was markedly different from Jethro's notion of a multi-layered hierarchy of rulers.

(2) Do not the Old Testament figures of Moses, Joshua, David, Solomon, etc. show that God's perfect will is to have a single leader over His people?

No, they do not. Moses and every other single leader in the Old Testament were shadows of the Lord Jesus Christ. They were not types of the modern-day single pastorate that was invented during the Reformation.

To be more specific, the role of the monarchical episcopate goes back to nascent (beginning) Catholicism. It finds its roots in the teachings of Ignatius of Antioch and Cyprian of Carthage. But it did not became widely accepted until the third and fourth centuries. During the Reformation the role of bishop and priest were transformed into the Protestant pastor.

By contrast, God's idea had always been to instill a theocracy in Israel. A theocracy is a government where God is the sole King. Yet while the Lord succumbed to the people's fleshly desire to have an earthly king, this was never His perfect will (1 Sam. 8:5-9).

Granted, the Lord still worked with His people under a human kingship. But they suffered dire consequences as a result. In like manner, God still works through imperfect systems today. Yet they always limit His full working.

The Lord's full desire for Israel was that she live and serve under His direct reign (Ex. 15:18; Num. 23:21; Deut. 33:5; 1 Sam. 8:7); that she be a kingdom of priests (Exod. 19:6); and that she be subject to older, wiser men (elders) in times of crisis (Deut. 22:15-18; 25:7-9).

But what Israel lost in her disobedience, the church gained (1 Pet. 2:5,9; Rev. 1:6). Tragically, however, many Christians have opted to return to the old covenant system of religious government—even though God dismantled it long ago. It is only because of an indwelling Spirit that God's idea of leadership and authority can be fulfilled today. Since the indwelling Spirit was not experienced during Old Testament days, God condescended to the limitations of His people. It is for this reason that we often see Israel embracing hierarchical leadership patterns. Yet when we come to the NT era, we learn that the indwelling Christ is the portion of all of God's children. And it is that portion that causes the church to rise to the supernatural level of "the priesthood of all believers." A level where hierarchical, titular, and official leadership styles turn obsolete and counter-productive.

(3) In Psalm 105:15, the Lord says "Touch not mine anointed, and do my prophets no harm." Doesn't this verse teach that some Christians (e.g., prophets) have unquestioned authority?

Under the Old Covenant, God specially anointed prophets to bear His oracles. To speak against them was to speak against the Lord. But under the New Covenant, the Spirit has been poured out upon *all* of God's people. All who have received Christ (the Anointed One) are anointed by the Holy Spirit (1 John 2:27)—and all may prophesy (Acts 2:17-18; 1 Cor. 14:31).

In this way, the prayer of Moses that all of God's people would receive the Spirit and prophesy has been fulfilled since Pentecost (Num. 11:29; Acts 2:16-18). Regrettably, Psalm 105:15 has been abused and misapplied by clergy leaders and self-proclaiming "prophets" to control God's people and to deflect criticism.

But here is the truth. Since all Christians have been anointed with the Spirit, all may prophesy (Acts 2:17-18; 1 Cor. 14:31). Under the New Covenant, "touch not God's anointed" is the equivalent of "subject yourselves to *one another* in the fear of Christ" (Eph. 5:21). For the Spirit's anointing has come upon all who believe in the Messiah.

Therefore, "touch not God's anointed" applies to *every* Christian today! To deny this is to deny that all Christians have the anointing (1 John 2:20,27).

The Problem of Mistranslation

In view of the foregoing points, some may wonder why the Authorized Version (KJV) obscures so many texts that have to do with ministry and oversight. In other words, why does the KJV repeatedly insert hierarchical/institutional terms (like "office") that are absent from the original documents?

The answer stems from the fact that the Anglican church of the 17th century issued the KJV. This church rigidly espoused the wedding of the Church and the State. It possessed a mindset that merged officialdom with Christianity.

Here is the story. King James VI of Scotland ordered the translation that bears his name (the King James Version). In doing so, the king acted in the capacity of the head of the Anglican church—the state church of England. He then directed the fifty-four scholars who authored the translation not to depart from "traditional terminology" throughout the project (*The Christian Baptist, Volume 1*, Nashville: The Gospel Advocate Co., 1955, pp. 319-324).

For this reason, the KJV naturally reflects Anglicanism's hierarchical/institutional presuppositions. Words like *ekklesia*, *episkopos*, and *diakonos* were not accurately translated from the Greek. Instead, they were translated into the Anglican ecclesiastical jargon of the day: *Ekklesia* = church. *Episkopos* = bishop. *Diakonos* = minister. *Praxis* = office. *Proistemi* = rule. The original KJV of 1611 went through four revisions up until 1769. Yet these errors were never corrected.

Thankfully, some modern translations have sought to correct this problem. They have de-Anglicized many of the ecclesiastical terms found in the KJV. They have also accurately translated the Greek words that stand behind them according to their native meanings: *Ekklesia* = assembly. *Episkopos* = overseer. *Diakonos* = servant. *Praxis* = function. *Proistemi* = guard.

Unfortunately, many translations still retain the official flavor present in the KJV. It is for this reason that I have written this chapter.

CHAPTER 3

AUTHORITY AND SUBMISSION

We have seen that there is no Biblical support for the modern "covering" teaching. Yet Scripture does have something to say about authority and submission. It should be noted, however, that the Bible spills far more ink in telling us how to love and serve one another than it does in teaching us about leadership and authority.

My experience has been that when the fundamental aspects of love and servanthood are mastered in a church, the issues of authority and submission amazingly take care of themselves. (In this connection, those who put undue emphasis on these subjects are typically more interested in making *themselves* an authority figure than they are in serving their brethren!)

So while the Bible does not make a lot of noise about authority and submission, the subjects are present. And they are germane to bearing ministry, receiving ministry, and pleasing Christ—the Head of all authority.

When we discuss these issues we do well to employ the vocabulary of Scripture. Using unbiblical jargon like "covering" only obscures the issue. It makes our conversation cluttered—our thoughts murky. If we stay with a NT vocabulary, we will be better able to cut through the matted layers of human tradition that have clouded the subjects of authority and submission.

The Tragic Trace of Past Movements

I am going to be blunt. Most of what passes today for "spiritual authority" is sheer folly! The discipleship/shepherding movement of the 1970s is a classic example of the unspeakable tragedies that occur when bogus and foolish applications of authority are made. This movement was riddled with spiritual mixture. And it degraded into extreme forms of control and manipulation.

The major error of the movement rested upon the false assumption that submission is the equivalent of unconditional obedience. Equally flawed was the teaching that God vests certain people with unquestioned authority over others.

To be sure, the leaders of this movement were gifted men with noble motives. They did not envision the direction that the movement would take. Most of them have since apologized for their role in spawning it. Even so, countless lives were devastated as a result.

In many segments of the movement spiritual abuse was rationalized under the oft-repeated platitude that God works good despite the actors in the cast. God, it was taught, will hold individual "shepherds" responsible for wrong decisions. The "sheep" bear no responsibility so long as they (mindlessly) obey their shepherds.

Tragically, the movement constructed new yokes of control that were whittled and shaped to fit the clerical caste. These new yokes suffocated the believing priesthood. And they exhibited the same domination of souls that characterize the cults. So-called "shepherds" were transformed into God-surrogates for other Christians, seizing control over the most intimate details of their lives. All of this was done in the name of "Biblical accountability."

In the aftermath, the movement left a trail of broken and disillusioned Christians. These believers continue to mistrust any semblance of leadership today. (Some suffered crueler fates.) As a result, those who were clergy-whipped in the movement developed an aversion to words like "authority," "submission," and "accountability." Even today, they still struggle to discard the distorted images of God that were etched in their minds by their "shepherding" experience.

The subject of authority, therefore, represents a sensitive and highly charged history for many. So much so, that when leadership terminology is merely uttered, alert lights go off and the red flag of victimization is raised.

Thirty years later, spiritual authority continues to be an emotionally laden and flammable subject. Despite the highly divergent take on the issue that is contained in this chapter, we are nonetheless treading on the edges of a hazardous minefield.

Keep in mind that erroneous teachings never spring from the mere employment of Biblical words. They rather stem from running roughshod over what they meant to their original hearers. Words like "authority" and "subjection" have been debased for so long that they need to be "redeemed" from the bogus connotations that have been attached to them.

So the safeguard to false teaching is not found in discarding these Biblical terms. It is rather found in rising above the fray and recasting them according to their original renderings. To put it another way, we must learn to not only speak *where* the Bible speaks. We must learn to speak *as* the Bible speaks.

The NT Notion of Subjection

The Greek word most often translated "submit" in the NT is the word *hupotasso*. *Hupotasso* is better translated "subjection." In its NT usage, subjection is a voluntary attitude of giving in, cooperating with, and yielding to the admonition and advice of another.

Biblical subjection has nothing to do with control or hierarchical power. It is simply an attitude of childlike openness in yielding to others insofar as they reflect the mind of the Lord.

Biblical subjection exists and it is precious. But it must begin with what God wants and what the NT assumes: Namely, that we are individually and corporately subject to Jesus Christ. That we are subject to one another in the place where we fellowship. And that we are subject to those proven and trustworthy workers who sacrificially serve the Body of Christ.

I stress "proven and trustworthy" for false prophets and false apostles abound. It is the responsibility of the local brethren to examine those who claim to be workers (1 Thess. 1:5; 2 Thess. 3:10; Rev. 2:2). For this reason, the Bible exhorts us to subject ourselves to spiritual leaders because of their noble character and spiritual service (1 Cor. 16:10-11,15-18; Phil. 2:29-30; 1 Thess. 5:12-13; 1 Tim. 5:17; Heb. 13:17).

Perhaps the most luminous text to consider in this discussion is Ephesians 5:21:

And be subject TO ONE ANOTHER in the fear of Christ.
(NASB)

Peter echoes the same thought saying,

Yea, all of you be subject TO ONE ANOTHER, and be clothed with humility: for God resisteth the proud, but giveth grace to the humble. (1 Pet. 5:5)

The Bible never teaches "protective covering." Instead, it teaches *mutual subjection*. Mutual subjection rests upon the NT notion that all believers are gifted. And as such, they may all express Jesus Christ. Therefore, we are to be in subjection to *one another*.

Mutual subjection is equally rooted in the revelation of the Body of Christ. That is, Divine authority has been vested in the *entire* Body rather than to a particular section of it (Matt. 18:15-20; 16:16-19; Eph. 1:19-23). In God's ecclesiology, the *ekklesia* is a theocratic, participatory society where Divine authority is dispersed to all who possess the Spirit.

God has not deputized His authority to any individual or segment of the church. Instead, His authority resides in the entire community. As the members of the believing community discharge their ministries, spiritual authority is dispensed through Spirit-endowed gifts.

At bottom, mutual subjection demands that we realize that we are members of something larger than ourselves—a Body. It also demands that we acknowledge that we are inadequate in ourselves to fulfill God's highest purpose.

Mutual subjection rests upon the humble, yet realistic affirmation that we need the input of our fellow brethren. It admits that we cannot be good Christians by ourselves. In this way, mutual subjection is indispensable to the texture of a normal Christian life.

Understanding mutual subjection means the following: It means you are open for the Lord to correct you through any believer. It means you are open to receive admonition and chastisement (from the Lord) regardless of who may hold the whip. It means you allow others to speak into your life.

God's Idea of Authority

The flip side of subjection is authority. Authority is God-given privilege to carry out a particular action. The NT word that is closest to our word "authority" is *exousia*. *Exousia* is derived from the word *exestin*. It means a possible and rightful action that can be carried out without hindrance.

Authority (*exousia*) has to do with the interpretation and communication of power. More specifically, authority is the right to carry out a particular action. Scripture teaches that God is the sole source of all authority (Rom. 13:1). And this authority has been vested in His Son (Matt. 28:18; John 3:30-36; 17:2).

Jesus Christ alone possesses authority. The Lord plainly said that "*all* authority is given to me in heaven and in earth." At the same time, God has delegated His authority to men and women in this world for specific purposes.

For instance, in the natural order of things, God has instituted various and sundry spheres in which His authority is exercised (Eph. 5:22-6:18; Col. 3:18-25). He has established certain "official authorities" which are designed to keep order under the sun. Governmental officials like kings, magistrates, and judges are given such authority (John 19:10,11; Rom. 13:1ff.; 1 Tim. 2:2; 1 Pet. 2:13-14).

Official authority is authority vested in a static office. It works regardless of the actions of the person who populates the office. Official authority is fixed, positional authority. As long as the person holds office, he has authority.

When authority is officiated to someone, the recipient becomes "an authority" in his own right. It is for this reason that Christians are charged to be subject to governmental leaders—regardless of their character (Rom. 13:1ff.; 1 Pet. 2:13-19).

Our Lord Jesus, as well as Paul, exhibited the spirit of subjection when they stood in the presence of official authority (Matt. 26:63-64; Acts 23:2-5). In like manner, we are always to be subject to such authority. Lawlessness and the despising of authority are marks of the sinful nature (2 Pet. 2:10; Jude 8). At the same time, subjection and obedience are two very different things. It is a fatal error to confuse them.

Subjection vs. Obedience

How does subjection differ from obedience? Subjection is an attitude. Obedience is an action. Subjection is absolute. Obedience is relative. Subjection is unconditional. Obedience is conditional. Subjection is an internal matter. Obedience is an external matter.

God summons us to have a spirit of humble subjection toward those whom He has placed in authority in the natural order. Yet we must not obey them if they command us to do that which violates His will. For the authority of God is higher than any earthly authority.

However, one can disobey while submitting. You can disobey an earthly authority while maintaining a spirit of humble subjection. You can disobey while having an attitude of respect and reverence as opposed to a spirit of rebellion, reviling, and subversion (1 Tim. 2:1-2; 2 Pet. 2:10; Jude 8).

The disobedience of the Hebrew midwives (Exod. 1:17); the three Hebrew young men (Dan. 3:17-18); Daniel (Dan.

6:8-10); and the apostles (Acts 4:18-20; 5:27-29) all exemplify the principle of being subject to official authority while disobeying it when it conflicts with God's will.

While God has established official authority to operate in the natural order, He has not instituted this kind of authority in the church. It is for this reason that ecclesiastical leaders are glaringly absent from Paul's discussion of the spheres of authority mentioned in Ephesians 5-6 and Colossians 3.

Granted, God has given believers authority *(exousia)* to exercise certain rights. Among them is the authority *(exousia)* to become the children of God (John 1:12); to own property (Acts 5:4); to decide to marry or live celibate (1 Cor. 7:37); to decide what to eat or drink (1 Cor. 8:9); to heal sickness and drive out devils (Matt. 10:1; Mark 3:15; 6:7; Luke 9:1; 10:19); to edify the church (2 Cor. 10:8; 13:10); to receive special blessings associated with certain ministries (1 Cor. 9:4-18; 2 Thess. 3:8-9); to govern nations and eat of the tree of life in the future kingdom (Rev. 2:26; 22:14).

The Bible never teaches that God has given believers authority *(exousia)* over other believers! Recall our Lord's word in Matthew 20:25-26 and Luke 22:25-26 where He condemned *exousia*-type authority forms among His followers. This fact alone should give us pause for serious reflection.

Therefore, it is a leap in logic and an over-extrapolation of reason to suggest that church leaders wield the same brand of authority as do dignitaries. Again, the NT never links *exousia* with church leaders. Nor does it ever state that some believers have *exousia* over other believers.

To be sure, the Old Testament portrays prophets, priests, kings and judges as official authorities. This is because these "offices" stood as shadows of the authoritative ministries of

Jesus Christ Himself. Christ is the real Prophet, Priest, King, and Judge. But never do we find any church leader described or depicted as an official authority in the NT. This includes local overseers as well as extra-local workers.

To be blunt, the notion that Christians have authority over other Christians is an example of forced exegesis. As such, it is Biblically indefensible. When church leaders wield the same type of authority that governmental officials do, they become usurpers!

Admittedly, authority does function in the church. But the authority that works in the *ekklesia* is strikingly different from the authority that works in the natural order. This only makes sense since the church is not a human organization, but a spiritual organism. The authority that operates in the church is not *official* authority. It is *organic* authority.

Official Authority vs. Organic Authority

What is organic authority? Organic authority is authority that is based on spiritual life. Organic authority is *communicated* authority. That is, when a person communicates God's life through word or deed they have the support and backing of the Lord Himself.

All Christians, by virtue of the fact that they have the life of the Spirit, possess a measure of organic authority. This is why the NT enjoins us to subject ourselves to *one another* in the fear of Christ. But those who are more seasoned in spiritual life tend to express God's thought more consistently than the carnal and the immature (Heb. 5:14).

Organic authority finds its source in Christ's *immediate* direction rather than in a static office. Organic authority is not intrinsic to a person or a position. It does not reside in man himself or in an office that he holds (as is the case with official authority).

Instead, organic authority is outside of the individual. This is because it belongs to Christ. Only when Christ directs a person to word or action does that person exercise authority. Put another way, a person has the right to be heard and obeyed only when he reflects the Lord's mind. Organic authority, therefore, is communicative and derivative.

The communicative nature of organic authority can be understood within the framework of the Body metaphor that Paul draws for the church. When the Head (who is the source of all authority) signals the hand to move, the hand possesses the authority of the Head. The hand, however, has no authority in itself. It derives authority only when it acts in accordance with the communication of the Head. Insofar as the hand represents the will of the Head, to that degree the hand is an authority.

Note that the movement of the physical head in relation to the physical body is organic. It is based on the human as a living organism of natural life. The same principle holds true for the spiritual Head and the spiritual Body. Believers only exercise spiritual authority when they are representing Christ in their words and deeds.

Organic authority, therefore, is flexible and fluid. It is not static. Organic authority is transmitted, not innovative. It is based upon spiritual life and service. So it is not an irrevocable possession.

This explains why Peter and James, as well as Paul and Barnabas, fluctuated with respect to the measure of spiritual authority they exerted (Acts 1:15; 2:14; 12:17,25; 13:2,7,13ff.; 15:2,7,13,22). Because organic authority is not officiated but derived, believers do not assume, inherit, confer, or substitute God's authority. They merely represent it. This is a blunt distinction. Failure to understand it has led to untold confusion and abuse among God's people.

When discussing spiritual authority the emphasis ought always to be on *function* and *service* rather than on a mystical notion of "spirituality." Claiming authority on the basis of one's spirituality is practically the same as making oneself an official authority. For the *claim* to "spirituality" constitutes a veiled office.

If one is truly spiritual, his spirituality will be manifested in how he lives, serves, and hears the Lord. Spirituality can only be discerned by the latter and not by the touted claims of the person who assumes it. In this way, keeping the focus on service and function helps protect NT-styled churches against devolving into personality cults.

A Helpful Comparison

Let us isolate some of the differences between official authority and organic authority.

1. Official authorities must be obeyed as long as what they declare does not violate the will of a higher authority (Acts 5:29). The NT advises children to obey their parents (Eph. 6:1; Col. 3:20), citizens to obey their governmental rulers (Titus 3:1), and employees to obey their employers (Eph. 6:5; Col. 3:22).

By contrast, those exercising organic authority never demand obedience to themselves. They rather seek to *persuade* others to obey God's will. For this reason Hebrews 13:17 summons us to allow ourselves to be persuaded (*peitho*) by our leaders.

Paul's letters throw further light on the subject. They all resonate with appeals and pleas. They are littered with the language of persuasion. (More on this later.)

2. Official authorities bear full responsibility when they lead those who are under them into wrong practices. In Numbers 18, we learn that the burden of iniquity fell upon the shoulders of the priests. They were official authorities in Israel.

By contrast, organic authority never nullifies the responsibility of others. In the church, believers bear full responsibility for their actions—even when they choose to obey the counsel of another.

It is for this reason that Scripture gives multiple injunctions to test the fruit of others. It equally teaches that deception brings Divine judgment (Matt. 7:15-27; 16:11-12; 24:4-5; 1 Cor. 14:29; Gal. 1:6-9; 2:4; Phil. 3:2-19; 1 Thess. 5:21; 1 Tim. 2:14; 1 John 3:4-10; 4:1-6). The NT never teaches that if a Christian obeys another person, he is no longer responsible for his actions.

3. Official authorities may be less mature, less spiritual, and less righteous than those over whom they have authority. Organic authority, however, is directly linked to spiritual maturity. It cannot be separated from it.

We often tell our children "obey your elders" because those who are older (in natural life) tend to be more mature in their counsel. Thus they deserve our respect and subjection (1 Pet. 5:5a). It is the same in the spiritual realm.

Those who have grown further in spiritual life bear a greater measure of organic authority. (A person cannot exercise spiritual authority unless he himself is under God's authority.) A sure sign of greater spiritual maturity is a spirit of servanthood and childlike meekness. Consider the following texts that exhort us to esteem those who display both characteristics:

> *Now I urge you, brethren (you know the household of Stephanas, that they were the first fruits of Achaia, and that they have devoted themselves for ministry to the saints), that you also BE IN SUBJECTION TO SUCH MEN AND TO EVERYONE WHO HELPS IN THE WORK AND LABORS. And I rejoice over the presence of Stephanas, and Fortunatus, and Achaicus; because they have supplied what was lacking on your part. For they have refreshed my spirit and yours. THEREFORE ACKNOWLEDGE SUCH MEN. (1 Cor. 16:15-18, NASB)*

> *Therefore receive him [Epaphroditus] in the Lord with all joy, and HOLD MEN LIKE HIM IN HIGH REGARD; BECAUSE HE CAME CLOSE TO DEATH FOR THE WORK OF CHRIST, RISKING HIS LIFE . . . (Phil. 2:29-30a, NASB)*

> *And we ask you, brethren, to KNOW THOSE LABOURING AMONG YOU, and leading you in the Lord, and admonishing you, and to ESTEEM THEM VERY ABUNDANTLY IN LOVE, BECAUSE OF THEIR WORK . . . (1 Thess. 5:12-13, Young's Literal Translation)*

> *Let the elders who take the lead among the saints well BE ESTEEMED WORTHY OF DOUBLE HONOUR, SPECIALLY THOSE LABOURING IN WORD AND TEACHING . . . Against an elder receive not an accusation unless where there are two or three witnesses. (1 Tim. 5:17,19, Young's Literal Translation)*

> *Remember those who led you, WHO SPOKE THE WORD OF GOD TO YOU; and CONSIDERING THE RESULT OF THEIR CONDUCT, IMITATE THEIR FAITH. (Heb. 13:7, NASB)*

Be obedient to [Greek: persuaded by] those leading you, and
BE SUBJECT, FOR THESE DO WATCH FOR YOUR SOULS,
AS ABOUT TO GIVE ACCOUNT, that with joy they may do
this, and not sighing, for this is unprofitable to you. (Heb.
13:17, Young's Literal Translation)

You younger men, likewise, BE SUBJECT TO YOUR ELDERS
. . . (1 Pet. 5:5, NASB)

Clearly, the NT exhorts the church to give weight to those
who tirelessly labor in spiritual service. Such esteem is both
spontaneous and instinctive. And it ought never to be
absolutized or formalized.

The NT criteria for role models is always functional, not
formal. While we should value the service of those who lay
their lives down for us, it is a grave mistake to mark them
off formally from the rest of the believing community. (This
is where the "covering" teaching goes wrong!)

Indeed, the honor that a believer receives from the church
is always merited. It is never demanded or asserted. Those
who are truly spiritual do not claim to have spiritual
authority over others. Nor do they boast about their spiritual
labor and maturity. In fact, people who make such claims
reveal their *immaturity*! The person that declares that he is
"God's anointed man of strength and power for the
hour"—or similar accolades—proves one thing: He has no
authority!

Contrarily, those who receive esteem in the church are
those who have *proven* themselves to be trustworthy servants. Not in mere rhetoric, but in reality (2 Cor. 8:22; 1
Thess. 1:5; 2 Thess. 3:10). Earned recognition and trust
from the Body is the only safe mark of one's spiritual authority.

4. Official authorities possess their authority until they are removed from their delegated office. As long as they hold office, their authority works regardless of whether they make unwise or unrighteous decisions. For example, as long as King Saul sat on Israel's throne, he retained his authority. This was true even after the Spirit of God departed from him (1 Sam. 16:14; 24:4-6)!

Organic authority, on the other hand, operates only when Christ is being expressed. So if a believer exhorts the church to do something that does not reflect the will of the Head (even if it may not violate a prescribed law of God), there is no authority to back him. Only Jesus Christ has authority. And only that which flows from His life carries authority.

5. Official authorities are virtually always set in a hierarchy. Organic authority is never related to hierarchy (Matt. 20:25-28; Luke 22:25-27). In fact, organic authority is always distorted and abused when allied with hierarchy. As we have already seen, hierarchical imagery is absent from Scripture. For it virtually always hurts God's people.

In short, organic authority does not flow from the top down. Nor does it function in a chain-of-command, hierarchical mode. At the same time, organic authority does not work from the bottom up. That is, it does not flow from the church to the person. For even if a church decides to give someone authority for a specific task, it lacks authority if it does not reflect the mind of Christ.

Organic authority works from *the inside out*. When the indwelling Christ leads a believer or a church to speak or act, they are backed by the authority of the Head! His is the only authority that exists in the universe. Jesus Christ, as represented by the indwelling Spirit, is the exclusive wellspring, mainstay, and source of all authority. And there is no covering over His Head!

The upshot is that leadership problems in the modern church stem from an obscenely simplistic application of official authority structures to spiritual relationships. This faulty application is rooted in a one-size-fits-all mentality of authority. But it is a profound mistake to transplant official authority into the Christian assembly—or into any other sphere of organic relationship (such as marriage).

Mutual Subjection is Always Framed in Love

Whenever a believer is expressing organic authority in the church, we do well to recognize it. To rebel against such authority is to rebel against Christ. For there is no authority without Jesus Christ as its Author. Consequently, to reject someone's words when they are expressing God's thought is to reject His authority.

While spiritual subjection is rooted in our submission to God, it is also framed in love. Love is always open to learn from and listen to what others have to say. At the same time, love is willing to admonish others when they falter.

Love rejects free-lancing, do-it-yourself, lone-star spirituality. It rather values the interdependence of the Body. Love realizes that because we are members one of another and have the same ancestry, our actions have a profound effect on others. Love deplores individualistic, privatized Christianity. But it affirms its need for the other members of Christ.

Love is sometimes sweet, kind, and nice. Yet when it faces the horrors of sin, it can be probing, combative, and unbending. Love is patient, respectful, and gentle. It is never strident, demeaning, or dictatorial. Love repudiates pompous and inflated claims to authority. Instead, it is profoundly stamped with humility and meekness.

Love is not flabby or sentimental, but keenly perceptive and discerning. Love offers to use its resources to help others. It never manipulates or imposes its own will. Love never forces, demands, or coerces.

Love propels us to accept responsibility in being our "brother's keeper." But it forbids us from becoming intrusive meddlers into their lives. Indeed, we are called to *represent* the Holy Spirit's will to one another. Yet we are never called to *substitute* His Person or *replace* His work!

Mutual subjection is not a license to probe into the intimate affairs of our fellow brethren to "make sure" they are walking aright! The Bible never gives us liberty to quiz our brethren about their financial investments, how they make love to their spouses, or other areas of intimacy.

This kind of unnecessary probing—exercised under the guise of "accountability"—is the stuff that authoritarian cults are made of. Such thinking will ultimately turn any believing community into a pressure-cooker of conformity. (Of course, if a believer *willingly desires* to confide in another about such personal matters, that is a different story. But that is a choice, not a duty.)

We must never lose sight of the fact that the Bible puts a high premium on individual Christian liberty, freedom, and privacy (Rom. 14:1-12; Gal. 5:1; Col. 2:16; Jas. 4:11-12). Therefore, respect for these virtues ought to be high among believers. Unless there is good reason to suspect that a brother or sister is in gross sin, it is profoundly unchristian to poke and pry into their domestic affairs.

The NT warns us against being "busybodies in other men's matters" . . . "speaking things that we ought not" (1 Tim. 5:13; 1 Pet. 4:15). By the same token, if a believer is in serious straits spiritually—struggling with some "grave sin"—love demands that he both seek and welcome help from the church.

In sum, because mutual subjection is always couched in love, it engenders a culture of spiritual safety and security. Mutual subjection is not control, but aid. It is never static or frozen into a formal system. It is not official, legal, or mechanical. It is rather functional, spontaneous, and organic. Danger looms whenever it is transformed into a human institution—no matter what name it flies under! As Christians, we have a spiritual instinct to submit to spiritual authority. And the church always benefits when we subject ourselves to it.

Whenever we welcome others to speak into our lives, we wedge the door open for the Lord to encourage, motivate, and protect us. It is for this reason that Proverbs repeatedly stresses that in "the *multitude of counselors* there is safety (Prov. 11:14; 15:22; 24:6). Love, then, is the Divine umbrella that affords spiritual protection. Yet thankfully, it is not as narrow as the hearts of some who are under its reach. In the final analysis, it is only love that has "covering" power (Prov. 10:12; 17:9; 1 Pet. 4:8).

The Cost of Mutual Subjection

Mutual subjection is radically different from unilateral subordination to authoritarian structures. At the same time, mutual subjection ought not to be confused with the highly individualistic, morally relative, tolerant egalitarianism that marks postmodern thinking.

Mutual subjection is costly. Let's face it. Our egos do not like being subject to anyone! As fallen creatures, we want to do what is right in *our own* eyes—without the interference of others.

The inclination to reject organic authority is deeply rooted in our Adamic nature (Rom. 3:10-18). Receiving correction, admonition, and reproof from other mortals constitutes a big cross to bear (Prov. 15:10; 17:10; 27:5-6; 28:23). It is for this reason that mutual subjection serves as an antidote to our rebellious flesh as well as to our lawless culture.

Exercising spiritual authority is equally painful. Unless one is a "control-freak," the task of reproving others is both difficult and risky. Scripture tells us that a brother who is offended is harder to be won than a walled city (Prov. 18:19)! Hence, the awkwardness of correcting others, coupled with the fear of confrontation, makes obeying the Lord in areas of expressing His authority hard on our flesh.

It is far easier to just let things go. It is far simpler to just pray for our "erring" brethren. It is far harder to lovingly confront them.

All of this just underscores the arresting fact that love is to govern our relationship with others. For if we love the brethren, we will subject ourselves to their counsel and admonition. Likewise, love compels us to approach our failing brethren in a spirit of meekness whenever they need our help (Gal 6:1; Jas. 5:19-20). At bottom, the way of love is always the way of the cross.

The Significance of Knowing God as Community

Because mutual subjection is framed in love, it is rooted in the very nature of the Godhead. God, by nature, is Community. The one God is made up of a Community of three Persons who eternally share their lives with one another. (This truth is historically referred to as *the Trinity*.)

Within the Godhead, the Father pours Himself into the Son. In turn, the Son gives Himself unreservedly to the Father. And the Spirit, as Mediator, pours their love from each to each. Within this Divine dance of love, there exists no hierarchy. There is only mutual fellowship, mutual love, and mutual subjection. (John 14:28 and 1 Cor. 11:3 do not contradict this principle. These texts have in view the voluntary subjection of the Son to the Father as His part of their relationship of mutual subjection.)

The mutual sharing that consistently occurs in the Godhead is the cornerstone of love. In fact, it is the very reason that John could say "God is love" (1 John 4:8). If God were not Community, there could have been no one for Him to love before creation. For the act of loving requires the presence of two or more persons.

The church is the community of the King. As such, it is called to mirror the reciprocal love relationship that occurs within the Godhead. There is no hierarchy in the Godhead. The same is true of the *ekklesia*. Within her walls there is only mutual subjection governed by mutual love. This is because the church lives by Divine life—the same life that exists in the Godhead (John 6:57; 17:20-26; 2 Pet. 1:4).

The NT is quite explicit in its use of the family motif for the church. The church is an extended family. A face-to-face community that shares one another's burdens, confesses sins to one another, and converses with one another over pending decisions. Within the family environment of the church, mutual subjection creates unity. It builds love. It provides stability. It fosters growth. And it gives a richer meaning to Christian living.

To put it another way, the Christian life was never meant to be lived outside of a face-to-face community. Nor can it be rightly lived out in any other environment. The *ek-*

klesia—the community of the King—is the Christian's natural habitat.

By contrast, in hierarchies, subjection and accountability are punitive and legalistic. They produce fear, domination, and control—things that were foreign to the early church.

In this way, mutual subjection is an antiseptic against hard-line Nicolaitanism (clericalism). For mutual subjection emphasizes power *for* and power *among* rather than power *over*. It encourages the empowerment of all rather than the power of a few. It stresses relationship rather than programs. Bonding rather than detachment. Connectedness rather than isolation. Organism rather than organization. Participation rather than spectatorship. Wholeness rather than fragmentation. Solidarity rather than individualism. Servitude rather than dominance. Interdependence rather than independence. And enrichment rather than insecurity.

While our culture encourages self-reliance, individualism, and independence, these things are incompatible with the ecology of the NT church. Because God is Community, His children are designed for community. Our new nature (through regeneration) calls out for it.

We Christians are not isolated beings. Like the Triune God who we were created after, our species is communal (Eph. 4:24; Col. 3:10). We thrive on meaningful relationships with others of the same kind. The modern "covering" doctrine obscures this unearthing insight. But the principle of mutual subjection brings it into sharp relief.

Stated simply, the Trinitarian nature of God serves as both the source and the model for all human community. And it is within the love relationship of the Godhead that the principle of mutual subjection finds its true value.

Mutual subjection, therefore, is not a human concept. It rather stems from the communal and reciprocal nature of the eternal God. And it is that very nature that the *ekklesia* is called to bear. In this way, mutual subjection enables us to behold the face of Christ in the very fabric and texture of church life.

To borrow the language of John Howard Yoder, the view of authority and submission presented in this chapter can be summed up thusly: "It gives more authority to the church than does Rome, trusts more to the Holy Spirit than does Pentecostalism, has more respect for the individual than Humanism, makes moral standards more binding than Puritanism, and is more open to the given situation than 'The New Morality.'"

CHAPTER 4

DENOMINATIONAL COVERING

The modern denominational system has made division in the Body of Christ acceptable. Many Christians believe that the denominations protect us from error. But this is an illusion.

"Denominational covering" is built on the superstitious idea that if I belong to a Christian denomination, I am somehow magically "covered" and "protected" from error. Yet the fact that people in the denominational system routinely "go off the beam" is proof that this idea is a charade. Therefore, the notion that I am "covered" by tracing my accountability to a top-down organization or a remote individual (like the Roman Catholic church traces its accountability to the pope) is pure fiction!

The only protection from error is in submitting ourselves to the Spirit of truth in the Body of Christ (1 John 2:20,27). God's idea of accountability works from person-to-people. Not from *parson*-to-person! Spiritual protection comes from relatedness to the Holy Spirit and spiritual connectedness with other Christians. Therein lies the genius of Christian community.

By contrast, the complicated, legalized, over/under system of denominational accountability is a man-made substitute for mutual subjection. To put it bluntly, denominationalism obscures mutual subjection in the fog of modern clericalism and in the heat of factional debates.

The Tyranny of the Status Quo

If you doubt that the denominational system is built on top-down control, try questioning it. If you do, be prepared to kick in the rhetoric engines of the clergy. For you will see sparks fly.

The frightening truth is that people who raise questions about ecclesiastical authority send tremors through the religious system. And they are often vilified as a result.

If you are one of them, prepare to be branded "a heretic," "a boat-rocker," "a trouble-maker," "a loose canon," or "an insubmissive rebel." Such invocation of the religious rhetoric is designed to stifle thought. It is calculated to derail honest dissent with the partisan status quo.

Accordingly, God's house still suffers from those who are fueled by a censorious spirit. It suffers from those who drive the Lord's precious ones out of His synagogue. And it suffers from those who shut the door to family members (3 John 9-10).

Those who usurp authority can wax eloquent about how they are safeguarding God's sheep from the perils of isolation. Granted, cults are perennially spawned because some isolate themselves from the Body of Christ. But here is the irony: The denominations do this very thing!

"Denominational covering" is very much like the skewed, master/slave notion of leadership that marks modern cults. In the denominations, members unreservedly follow a single leader or organization. By contrast, the Biblical principle of mutual subjection emphasizes submission to *one another* as opposed to unquestioned obedience to a human leader or hierarchical organization.

To put an even finer point on it, the "covering" teaching is often used as a bludgeon to dismiss those Christians who do not meet under a denominational flag. "Covering" constitutes a weapon in the hands of partisan religious groups to secure the theological terrain. This weapon is fueled by sectarian bigotry. And it has the net effect of fracturing the fellowship of God's people—slashing the Body of Christ into pieces—and carving the church into splintered fragments.

In a word, the modern denominational morass has polluted the Christian landscape. It has turned the "one Body" into a tragically divided, tradition-choked entity. Advocates of denominationalism believe that this system is helpful. To their minds, the different denominations represent the different parts of the Body of Christ.

But the denominational system is foreign to the NT! It is incompatible with Christian oneness. It is based on human divisions that are Biblically unjustifiable (1 Cor. 1-3). In effect, denominationalism stems from a fractured vision of the Body of Christ. (See my book, *Rethinking the Wineskin,* for further details.)

The Governing "Mother Church"

Every church born within the first seventeen years of Pentecost was spawned from the Jerusalem church. But these new churches had neither a formal nor a subservient relationship to Jerusalem. In this regard, the NT *always* envisions autonomous (independent) but fraternally related churches.

This means that in God's thought, every church is one in life with all other churches. But every church is independent, self-governing, and responsible to God alone for its decision-making. Hence, the concept of a governing "mother church" or a denominational headquarters is based on a wooden interpretation of Scripture. It is also grossly partisan!

It was never our Lord's desire that local churches attach themselves to a denominational headquarters, a super-federation, or a diocesan association. Scriptural principle affirms that each church is independent in its decision-making and oversight. (Consider our Lord's words to the seven churches of Asia. He dealt with each assembly according to its unique problems—Rev. 1-3.)

This principle is also underscored in Paul's letters. Paul consistently treats each church as an autonomous, self-governing organism. To Paul's mind, each church is directly responsible to God and directly accountable to Him (Eph. 5:24; Col. 1:9-10).

Therefore, it is a gross mistake to spin local churches together with the thread of religious federationism. The truth is that every church stands under the same Head. They are all one in life. Consequently, churches should cooperate with, learn from, and help one another (Acts 11:28-30; Rom. 15:25-29; 2 Cor. 8:1-14; 1 Thess. 2:14). This was the practice of the early churches (Rom. 16:1; 1 Cor. 16:19; 2 Cor. 13:13; Phil. 4:22).

At the same time, each church is obligated to embrace the tradition the apostles established for "every church" (1 Cor. 4:16-17; 7:17; 11:16; 14:33; 16:1; 1 Thess. 2:14). It is a departure from Divine principle, therefore, for a church to strike out on *purely* individualistic lines when it comes to ecclesiastical practices. The institutional church has done this very thing. It has invented a plethora of religious practices that violate NT principles.

According to Divine principle, each church should develop its own oversight, ministry, and unique testimony.

On the other hand, there should be spiritual relatedness and help among the churches.

Each church is directly responsible to its Head (Christ) and is under His immediate control. Each maintains a strong local independence in its affairs. This means, among other things, that it is unscriptural for a church to direct or discipline another church. Equally so, every church should receive help and encouragement from other churches.

In God's thought, a church does not have the right to regulate, control, or intrude upon the affairs, teachings, or practices of another assembly. The denominational system violates all of these principles.

So the unity and relatedness of churches preserve the testimony that *the Body* is one. And the independence and autonomy of churches preserve the testimony that *the Head* is sovereign.

The Question of Acts 15

As a counter argument, some have sought to tease out of Acts 15 a Biblical precedent for a governing "mother church." But a careful analysis of this text decisively shows that this is an unwarranted application that patently does not fit the rest of the NT. On the surface, it could appear that Paul and Barnabas went to the Jerusalem church because it had unilateral authority over every other church. However, this notion falls apart when the chapter is read in context.

Here is the story. Some from the Jerusalem church brought an erroneous teaching to the church in Antioch. Paul and Barnabas were prompted to pay Jerusalem a visit to settle the matter. Why? It was because the teaching had originated from Jerusalem (Acts 15:1-2, 24).

If the false teaching had come out of the Antioch church, Paul and Barnabas would have dealt with it there. But because the doctrine came from the Jerusalem church, the two men went to Jerusalem to determine who introduced the erroneous teaching. They also wanted to make sure the Jerusalem elders and the twelve apostles did not affirm it.

Upon their arrival, those in the church who taught the doctrine were identified (15:4-5). This led to a church council. The upshot was that the saints in Jerusalem repudiated the doctrine publicly (15:6ff.).

The decision reached by the council, which included the approval of the twelve apostles, the elders, and the whole church, was circulated to the Gentile churches. This was done in the advent that other churches could someday face the same troubling issue. Their decision carried God's authority because the Holy Spirit inspired it (15:28). And because the church affirmed it (15:23,28,31).

To read anything else into this story reflects a failure to take seriously the historical specifics behind the account. It is an example of reading one's own biases into the text rather than reading meaning and direction out of it. Consequently, the idea of an authoritative "mother church" lacks Scriptural merit. The first-century story will not hold it.

To be sure, the Jerusalem church was loved, appreciated, and helped by the other churches (Rom. 15:26-27; 2 Cor. 9:11-13). But there is nothing in the NT that would lead us to believe that it possessed supreme authority. Nor that all other churches were subservient to it. Rather, each church was autonomous and directly responsible to God. None were subordinate to any other.

The denominational system maps poorly to Scriptural example. It also violates spiritual principle. Denominationalism has fragmented the Body of Christ by religious partisanship. It has alienated the family of God. It has disintegrated the fabric of our spiritual brotherhood into an endless morass of religious parties. And it has spawned thousands of warring clans out of the one family of Christ.

Denominationalism is Self-Defeating

Another problem with the denominational system is that it crushes that which it claims to protect and preserve. It effectively *breaks* up that which it alleges to *build* up! Like the misguided sectarian zeal that drives Roman Catholicism, Protestant denominationalism has descended into a human institution that cracks the whip of despotism before its dissenters. It adeptly defends the party-line. And it damns others for alleged doctrinal trespasses.

It is for this reason that Paul thunders against the Corinthian Christians when they denominated and demarcated themselves into separate camps (1 Cor. 1:11-13; 3:3-4). That God's family today be pressed into the partisan straight jacket of demoninationalism is no less than scandalous. Incidentally, many so-called non-denominational, interdenominational, and post-denominational churches are just as sectarian and hierarchical as the mainline denominations. These also belong to "the denominational *system.*"

More striking, the denominational system actually perpetuates heresy—the very thing it claims to curb. Think about it. If the autonomous nature of every church were preserved, the spreading of error would be mostly localized. But when a denominational headquarters is infected with false teaching, every church connected with it embraces the same falsehood. Thus the heresy becomes widespread!

When every church is autonomous, it is difficult for an ambitious false teacher to emerge and seize control over a cluster of churches. It is also virtually impossible for a "pope-like figure" to emerge. Not so in a denomination. There all the related churches stand or fall together.

It can also be argued quite soundly that to form a denomination is to commit heresy. The sin of heresy [Greek: *hairesis*] is the act of choosing to follow one's own tenets. So a person can be a heretic with the truth if he uses it to fracture the Body of Christ. Denominations are formed when some split off from the larger Body of Christ to follow their favorite doctrines or practices.

While the institutional church makes its boast about being "covered" by a denomination, it actually affords less face-to-face accountability than modern first-century styled churches. In the typical evangelical church, the pastor is said to "cover" the congregation. But in most churches of this ilk, the bulk of the congregation barely knows the pastor! (Let alone one another!)

It is not uncommon for "churchgoers" to say less than three sentences to each other during a typical Sunday morning service. By contrast, in a NT-styled church, all the brethren know one another intimately. This includes the extra-local workers who help the church (1 Thess. 5:12a).

All in all, "denominational covering" is artificial. And it is confined to the safe limits of its own inherent shallowness. Contrarily, God's desire is that His people embody the values of His Son's life and teaching in an intimate, face-to-face community. In fact, this desire constitutes the very heartthrob of His eternal purpose (Eph. 2:18-3:11).

In a word, mutual subjection preserves the church as a close-knit, unified community. Denominational "covering" turns it into a hierarchical society!

A Word About Christian Orthodoxy

Clearly, the mere employment of traditional church structures like the pastor system of Protestantism, the priestly system of Roman Catholicism, and the denominational system of Christendom, can never safeguard the Lord's people from doctrinal error. Bracketing the raft of independent churches that have gone off the rails of Christian orthodoxy, many clergy-led denominations have followed in the same path. The Watchtower Society, the Way International, the Unification Church, the Church of Jesus Christ of the Latter-Day Saints are examples.

In addition to mutual subjection, historic Christian teaching on the essential doctrines of the faith plays a crucial role in keeping a church on Scriptural track. Throughout the centuries, Christians have preserved the core beliefs of our faith. These beliefs were hammered out into creedal statements in the midst of a plethora of doctrinal heresies.

Creeds like the Nicene Creed, the Apostles' Creed, etc. represent the unified voice of the historic church on the essentials of our faith. They attest to the fundamental truths of Christianity. Truths like Jesus Christ is God and man, He was born of a virgin, He was crucified for our sins, and He rose again in bodily form.

These creeds do not belong to any one ecclesiastical tradition or denomination. Instead, they are the heritage of all genuine believers. They adequately reflect the voice of the church throughout history. To be sure, the language used in these creeds is archaic. But their *meaning* mirrors sound Biblical teaching.

Put another way, the Ecumenical Creeds embody what C.S. Lewis called *Mere Christianity*—"the belief that has been common to nearly all Christians at all times." (An

earlier version of the same idea was put forth by Vincent of
Lerins in these words: "Christianity is what has been held
always, everywhere, and by all.")

While the creeds alone are not a sufficient deterrent for
lapsing into doctrinal error, they serve as warning signs
alerting us if we are straying from basic Christian teaching.

Although the creeds should not be viewed as perfect
theological statements, they function as historically tested
guideposts to our common faith. The creeds do not super-
sede Scripture. Nor are they beyond expansion or im-
provement. But when properly handled, they help safeguard
orthodoxy.

Accordingly, the historical creeds are helpful instruments
that our spiritual forefathers left to us in their quest to
faithfully follow Jesus Christ. It is a gross mistake, therefore, to blanketly disregard their contribution simply
because some of them were part of the "organized church"
of their day.

Let us not forget that the very canon of Scripture that we
all hold dear was both defended and formally compiled by
those within institutional church structures. This did not
prevent them from joining the voice of the apostles regarding God's sacred oracles. Keep in mind that the Body of
Christ includes *all* Christians from every age—irrespective
of the church structures to which they were a part.

So the call to recover the ecology of the NT church does
not include a summons to reinvent the religious wheel on
every theological issue. Nor does it include a rejection of all
that has been passed down to us by our spiritual forefathers.

Instead, it sides with every voice of the past that has
remained true to the apostolic revelation—no matter what
segment of the historic church to which they may have
belonged. The primitive church was rooted in the soil of

Christian truth. And staying within that soil requires that we stand on the shoulders of those who have gone before us.

CHAPTER 5

APOSTOLIC AUTHORITY

While a full-scale discussion of the ministry of the apostle is beyond the scope of this book, my treatment of the anatomy of apostolic authority affirms that apostles still exist today. Without doubt, the twelve apostles hold a unique place in God's economy (Luke 22:30; Rev. 21:14). (The twelve would include Matthias who replaced Judas Iscariot—Acts 1:26.)

Yet Scripture mentions other apostles beyond the twelve. Paul and Barnabas (Acts 14:4,14; 1 Cor. 9:1-6), James, the Lord's brother (Gal. 1:19), Timothy and Silas (1 Thess. 1:1; 2:6) are just some of the apostles that appear throughout the pages of the NT.

Apostolic ministry, therefore, continued beyond the death of the original twelve. It did not pass away after the first century. Neither was it transmitted formally through an institutional hierarchy.

While apostles are not writing Scripture today, they are still Divinely commissioned to build the Body of Christ (1 Cor. 12:28-29; Eph. 4:11). The chief work of an apostle is to raise up churches. This does not mean that a church cannot be birthed without the hand of an apostle. The churches of Syrian Antioch, Caesarea, Tyre, and Ptolemais do not appear to have been founded by one.

But all of these churches received help from an apostolic worker shortly after their births. In fact, *every* church in the

NT was either planted or greatly helped by an apostolic worker.

Apostolic workers do not establish missions, de-nominations, cell-groups, para-church organizations, or institutional "churches." They only plant *ekklesias* that are grounded and sustained by Jesus Christ—the Chief Architect of the church (1 Cor. 3:6-15).

Apostolic workers are gifted brethren who are specially commissioned by God to their work (Rom. 1:1; 1 Tim. 2:7; 2 Tim. 1:11). And they are approved and sent out to this work by those believers who know them intimately. Consider Acts 13:1-4:

> *Now there were at Antioch, in the church that was there, PROPHETS AND TEACHERS: Barnabas, and Simeon who was called Niger, and Lucius of Cyrene, and Manaen who had been brought up with Herod the tetrarch, and Saul. And while they were ministering to the Lord and fasting, the Holy Spirit said, "SET APART for me Barnabas and Saul for THE WORK to which I have called them." Then, when they had fasted and prayed and laid hands on them, they SENT THEM AWAY. So, being SENT OUT BY THE HOLY SPIRIT, they went down to Seleucia and from there they sailed to Cyprus.*

The commission of an apostolic worker is *personal*. But his sending out is *corporate*. An apostolic worker is usually a teacher, prophet, or evangelist who has been directly called by God to a regional work. He has also been publicly sent out by a local group of believers.

It is this inward commission and outward separation that constitutes one an apostolic worker. Workers can also be sent out by the hand of an older worker who mentors them (1 Cor. 4:17; 2 Cor. 8:16-23; 12:18; Eph. 6:21-22; Col. 4:7-8; 1 Thess. 3:1-2; 2 Tim. 4:12; Titus 3:12-13)

Significantly, the Greek word *apostolos*, which is translated "apostle," literally means one who is sent forth. Therefore, the NT knows nothing of a *self*-appointed, *self*-sent apostle.

Apostolic workers, in the NT sense, are those who are *sent*. They are itinerant, mobile, translocal people who critique the culture, proclaim the gospel, and plant and nurture *ekklesias*. Just how they accomplish these tasks and how much authority they possess are questions that we will consider in this chapter.

The Question of Apostolic Covering

Similar to "denominational covering," but having a flair all of its own, is the notion of "apostolic covering." The teaching of "apostolic covering" holds that a church is protected from doctrinal error if it submits to a contemporary apostle (=church planter). It rests upon the idea that apostolic workers have official authority to control and direct the affairs of a church.

The Bible, however, runs contrary to this idea. Nowhere in the NT do we find an apostle assuming the full responsibility of a local church once the foundation has been fully laid. Rather, the apostles of the NT both recognized and respected the spiritual autonomy of each church once they were established.

Granted, the church was in the hands of the worker while he was laying the foundation. But the responsibility fell into the hands of the church once he departed. And he *always* departed!

In the beginning of a church's life, the burden of oversight belongs to the apostolic worker. It then shifts to the elders once they emerge. Apostolic workers are responsible for their own regional ministries. The church is responsible for its own local affairs.

Again, when an apostolic worker is giving birth to a church, the church is in his hands. Such a period can be likened to an incubation phase. The worker spends time ministering Christ to the saints and equipping them for ministry. It is for this reason that Paul rented his own house to conduct apostolic meetings alongside the meetings of the church (Acts 28:30-31).

Paul did something similar when he was in Ephesus. He held apostolic meetings in the Hall of Tyrannus while the local believers gathered in homes (Acts 19:9; 20:20; 1 Cor. 16:19). Such apostolic meetings were meetings of *the work*. They were designed to equip the saints to function in *the church*.

But once the worker laid the foundation and left the saints on their own, he delegated all oversight and responsibility into the hands of the local believers. In this way, first-century apostles never settled down in a church to control its affairs. They always left.

While Paul sometimes spent an extended length of time to plant a church (Corinth 18 months; Ephesus 3 years), he always left those churches on their own once the foundation was established. And after leaving, he did not meddle in the church's affairs.

In like manner, Antioch served as Paul's home-base for his first two apostolic journeys. Yet he did not dominate the church's affairs while there. In Antioch, Paul was simply a respected brother. He was not an apostle to that church.

This explains why the NT mentions the elders of Ephesus, the elders of Jerusalem, the overseers of Philippi, etc. But it never mentions the apostles of these places. While the twelve resided in Jerusalem as a home-base for their ministry during the initial season of the church's existence, the NT never calls them "the apostles *of* Jerusalem." Yet the ministry of the apostolic workers complements the ministry of the churches.

The apostolic ministry, or "the work" (*ergon*) as the Bible calls it (Acts 13:2; 14:26; 15:38), exists as a separate entity from the churches. The work is regional. The churches are local. The work is transient. The churches are settled. The work is a roving *association*. The churches are resident *communities*. Apostolic workers are travelers, not settlers. They are pioneers, not stationaries.

A careful study of Paul's apostolic journeys reveals the striking fact that he usually spent very little time with the churches he planted. Typically, Paul would spend several months establishing the ground floor of a believing community, only to leave it to itself for lengthy periods of time. While away from them, he was available to offer advice (1 Cor. 7:1). He also made periodic visits to check on their progress and to strengthen them (Acts 15:36; 18:23; 2 Cor. 12:14; 13;1). But he never took charge of their affairs.

The practice of leaving the churches in their infancy reveals the daunting fact that Paul believed the church to be a living organism that would develop on its own by the power of God's life. He knew that when he left a church the Spirit would remain.

At the same time, the churches that Paul planted received help from other churches (Acts 16:2; 1 Thess. 1:7-8). They also stayed in steady contact with Paul. In fact, even after twelve years, the church in Philippi still needed the spiritual ministry of their founding apostle (Php. 1:23-27).

It is absolutely essential that modern house churches receive the ministry of apostolic workers to help them. When a church does not open its doors to outside help and deems itself *completely* "self-sufficient," it suffers tremendous loss. House churches, therefore, must avoid becoming islands unto themselves. To do so is spiritual suicide. (See my book *So You Want to Start a House Church?* for details.)

The work exists for the churches—not for its own sake. In fact, the work produces the churches. At the same time, the churches produce workers. (Every apostle in the first-century was *first* a well-known and trusted brother in a church before his sending out.) The work is never to rival, substitute, or overshadow the church. For the goal of the work is to establish and strengthen the churches.

In a word, apostolic workers are responsible for planting and nurturing churches in many different places. Genuine apostles never permanently settle down in the churches they plant. Nor do they assume exclusive authority over them. In this connection, the modern pastoral role is a distorted version of a *stationary* apostle. Such a creature is a spiritual oxymoron!

Church Planters or Church Supplanters?

Although apostles were valued servants to the early churches, they were not usurpers (1 Cor. 4:1). They did not conduct themselves as resident chairmen or distant bosses over the assemblies.

Put another way, the first-century apostles were church *planters*—not church *supplanters*! They were assistants, not spiritual aristocrats. Servants, not ecclesiastical despots. Foundation layers, not high-powered celebrity figures. While first-century apostles instructed and persuaded the churches, they never controlled them.

While some today have glamorized the apostolic vocation, Paul considered apostles to be *"fools . . . weak . . . without honor . . . the last of all . . . the scum of the world, the dregs of all things"(1 Cor. 4:9-13, NASB).* True workers, therefore, are not glory-grabbers. They do not seek to impress people (2 Cor. 11:5-6; 1 Thess. 2:5-6). They do not seek financial gain (2 Cor. 2:17; 11:9). Nor do they dominate the lives of others (2 Cor. 1:24).

True workers do not claim impressive credentials (2 Cor. 3:1-3). They do not assert a superior heritage (2 Cor. 11:21-22). Nor do they boast of extraordinary spiritual experiences (2 Cor. 10:12-15; 11:16-19; 12:1,12).

For Paul, apostolic workers are not self-appointed, self-styled, self-advancing, spiritual elitists. Rather, they are those who shovel the dung after the procession ends! They are those who spill their blood for the churches. Like all true leaders, genuine workers are always found quietly serving any and all who have need.

The grabbing of power and the exertion of oneself over others is not apostleship (sent-ness). It is just another stale, warmed over version of oppression. Real workers are first and foremost servants.

The seal of a true apostolic worker is simply this: he plants NT *ekklesias* that survive in his absence (1 Cor. 9:2; 2 Cor. 3:1-2). All of this is consistent with Paul's own practice—whose apostolic ministry is given the most attention in the NT.

Instead of deploying imperial metaphors, Paul draws metaphors from the family to describe his relationship to the churches he worked with. To the churches, Paul is a father, a mother, and a nurse (1 Cor. 3:2; 4:14-15; 2 Cor. 12:14; Gal. 4:19; 1 Thess. 2:7,11). He is not a lord, a master, or a king!

Likewise, the persuasive overtones that permeate Paul's letters show that he treated the churches as a father would treat his *adult* children as opposed to his toddlers. As a father, he gave his judgment on church affairs. But he did not issue unilateral decrees.

The letter of 1 Corinthians is a clear example of this tendency. It reaches its peak when Paul offers his judgment on handling a brother who is committing incest. He calls on the whole church to discipline him (1 Cor. 5:1-13).

In effect, the churches that Paul planted progressively moved away from dependence upon him. They rather grew in their dependence upon Christ (1 Cor. 2:1-5). And Paul urged them in this path (1 Cor. 14:20; Eph. 4:14).

The Pauline Method of Planting and Nurturing Churches

One of the most dynamic features of Paul's method of church planting was his consistent subjection to other Christians. From the outset of his conversion, Paul learned to depend upon the spiritual supply of his fellow brethren. His first lesson of subjection to the Body was with Ananias. Ananias was the brother at whose hands Paul received the Spirit and a confirmation of his calling (Acts 9:17-19; 22:12-16).

Subsequently, Paul was sent away by the believers in Berea (Acts 17:14). He was strengthened by his co-laborers in Corinth (Acts 18:5). He was restrained by the saints at Ephesus (Acts 19:30). He was also advised by the brothers at Jerusalem (Acts 21:23). In a word, Paul knew how to receive help and enrichment from others (Rom. 15:32; 1 Cor. 16:18; Phil. 2:19; 2 Tim. 1:16).

While he was certainly endowed with a seasoned spiritual history and many powerful gifts, Paul regarded his authority as functional and relational—not official or sacral. For Paul, spiritual authority was rooted in the Lord's approval, not in some formal office (2 Cor. 10:18).

This explains why Paul virtually always sought to *persuade* the churches concerning God's mind rather than issuing imperial commands. In fact, Paul's two favorite words for addressing the saints are *parakalein* and *erotao*. *Parakalein* means an appeal. *Erotao* means a request made between equals.

In the same strain, Paul refrained from using the very strong word *epitage* (=commandment) to charge obedience to himself. Consider the following texts:

But I speak this by permission, and NOT OF COM-MANDMENT. (1 Cor. 7:6)

Now concerning virgins I HAVE NO COMMANDMENT OF THE LORD: YET I GIVE MY JUDGMENT, as one that hath obtained mercy of the Lord to be faithful. (1 Cor. 7:25)

I speak NOT BY COMMANDMENT, but by occasion of the forwardness of others, and to prove the sincerity of your love. (2 Cor. 8:8)

Therefore, although in Christ I could be bold and order you to do what you ought to do, YET I APPEAL TO YOU ON THE BASIS OF LOVE. (Phlm. 8-9, NIV)

When Paul called the believers to action or attitude, we find him "urging," "beseeching," "pleading," "appealing," and "asking" rather than issuing authoritarian decrees. Paul's letters are dripping with this kind of cooperative tone. (See Rom. 12:1; 15:30; 16:2,17; 1 Cor. 1:10; 4:16;

16:12,15; 2 Cor. 2:8; 5:20; 6:1; 8:6; 9:5; 10:1-2; 12:18; Gal. 4:12; Eph. 3:13; 4:1; Phil. 4:2-3; 1 Thess. 2:3,11; 4:1,10; 5:12,14; 2 Thess. 2:1; 3:14-15; 1 Tim. 1:3; 2:1; Phlm. 9-10, 14.)

To Paul's mind, the voluntary consent of his audience and their internalization of truth was far more desirable than nominal obedience to the things he wrote. At times when his tone was needfully sharp, Paul charged the saints to commend obedience to Christ rather than to himself (Rom. 1:5; 16:19,26; 2 Cor. 2:9; Phil. 2:12).

On rare occasions he did charge (*paraggello*) obedience to the things that he had written (1 Thess. 4:11; 2 Thess. 3:4,6,10,14). But the object of obedience was not Paul as a person. It was Christ whose mind he was expressing at the time.

Put another way, whenever Paul manifested the mind of Christ, his words were *authoritative*. But Paul himself was never *authoritarian*! Consider the following texts:

I know and am persuaded BY THE LORD JESUS that there is nothing unclean of itself . . . (Rom. 14:14)

And unto the married I command, YET NOT I, BUT THE LORD . . . (1 Cor. 7:10)

If any man think himself to be a prophet, or spiritual, let him acknowledge that THE THINGS THAT I WRITE UNTO YOU ARE THE COMMANDMENTS OF THE LORD. (1 Cor. 14:37)

For we are not as many, which corrupt the word of God: but as of sincerity, BUT AS OF GOD, IN THE SIGHT OF GOD SPEAK WE IN CHRIST. (2 Cor. 2:17)

For we preach NOT OURSELVES, BUT CHRIST JESUS THE LORD; and ourselves your servants for Jesus' sake. (2 Cor. 4:5)

Again, think ye that we excuse ourselves unto you? WE SPEAK BEFORE GOD IN CHRIST: but WE DO ALL THINGS, DEARLY BELOVED, FOR YOUR EDIFYING. (2 Cor. 12:19)

Since ye seek A PROOF OF CHRIST SPEAKING IN ME, which to you-ward is not weak, but is mighty in you. For though he was crucified through weakness, yet he liveth by the power of God. For we also are weak in him, but WE SHALL LIVE WITH HIM BY THE POWER OF GOD TOWARD YOU. (2 Cor. 13:3-4)

For this cause also thank we God without ceasing, because, when ye received the word of God which ye heard of us, ye received it NOT AS THE WORD OF MEN, BUT AS IT IS IN TRUTH, THE WORD OF GOD . . . (1 Thess. 2:13)

For ye know what commandments we gave you BY THE LORD JESUS . . . (1 Thess. 4:2)

For THIS WE SAY UNTO YOU BY THE WORD OF THE LORD . . . (1 Thess. 4:15)

Now them that are such we command and exhort BY OUR LORD JESUS CHRIST . . . (2 Thess. 3:12)

So Paul was not an authoritarian personality. Nor was he an independent free-lancer. From his own lips, he made clear that he did not regard his apostolic calling a license to dominate the affairs of the churches. Paul never exploited his right as an apostle to receive financial help from those he served (1 Cor. 9:1-19).

In fact, his abiding principle was to refuse funds from those churches that he was serving at the time. Paul only accepted money from believers in other locales so as to not burden those who were recipients of his immediate help (2 Cor. 11:7-9).

In effect, Paul's whole outlook of apostolic authority is crystallized in the statement, *"Not that we have dominion over your faith, but are helpers of your joy . . . "* (2 Cor. 1:24). Eugene Peterson paraphrases this passage as follows: *We're not in charge of how you live out the faith, looking over your shoulders, suspiciously critical. We're partners, working alongside you, joyfully expectant. I know that you stand by your own faith, not by ours (The Message).*

In this way, Paul differed immeasurably from his opponents (2 Cor. 11:19-21).

The Source of Paul's Authority

The authority that Paul possessed was tied to his ability to speak the word of the Lord to the communities he founded. This is why it was an authority designed to "build up rather than to tear down" (2 Cor. 10:8; 13:10). Paul, therefore, always exercised authority for the sole purpose for which it was given—to edify the saints. He never misused it to gain prominence, earthly power, or material advantage.

Paul recognized that the source of his authority was Christ Himself as He is embodied in the gospel. This explains why he consistently invited the saints to judge what he said (1 Cor. 10:15; 11:13; 1 Thess. 5:21). Paul even urged the saints to reject his message if it was not consistent with the gospel (Gal. 1:8-9).

In like manner, the NT authors as a whole consistently exhort the churches to obey the raw truth of the gospel as it is found in Jesus Christ. The words of mere men are not to be obeyed at face value (Rom. 6:17; Gal. 3:1; 5:7; Titus 1:14).

Paul expected the churches to give him a hearing insofar as his words reflected the gospel of Christ (Gal. 1:9). And insofar as they were in harmony with the Spirit of God (1 Cor. 7:40). Indeed, Paul was forced to reprove the churches on occasion. But he always found this difficult to do.

His reticence for giving rebuke is disclosed in his Corinthian correspondence. There we discover that Paul preferred to come to them with a spirit of gentleness rather than with a word of reproof (1 Cor. 4:21b). Yet when he had to address them sternly, he did so with much anguish of heart (2 Cor. 2:4). (Incidentally, Paul's "rod" in 1 Cor. 4:21 is a metaphor for a word of rebuke rather than a token of forced subordination or unilateral authority—2 Cor. 10:3-6.)

Paul's love for the Corinthians was so overflowing with fatherly compassion that after he wrote them, he feared that his words may have been too strong (2 Cor. 7:8). Clearly, the consuming motivation that drove Paul to tirelessly labor and suffer for the churches was his surpassing love for their souls (2 Cor. 12:15; Phil. 2:17-21; Col. 1:24; 1 Thess. 2:8).

Because Paul often spoke the word of the Lord, he could say that those who rejected his words did not reject him but Christ (1 Thess. 4:8). For to Paul's mind, "God has given us His Holy Spirit" (4:8b). Yet even in those times where the word of the Lord was in his mouth, Paul willed that the believers acknowledge what he said to be the Lord's thought rather than his own (1 Cor. 14:37-38).

That Paul appealed to his faithful service as a basis for the saints' trust is unmistakable (1 Cor. 4:1-5; 7:25; 15:10; 2 Cor. 1:12; 4:1-2). Even so, Paul seemed more interested in having his converts imitate his walk rather than hear his words (1 Cor. 4:16; Gal. 4:12; Phil. 3:17; 4:9; 2 Thess. 3:7). Of course, the reason why Paul could present himself as a model for others to follow was because his life mirrored that of His Lord (Acts 20:34-35; 1 Cor. 11:1).

All of these facts embody the following sound insight: The *source* of spiritual authority is Christ. The *means* of spiritual authority is the Word of God. The *exercise* of spiritual authority is brokenness and servanthood. And the *goal* of spiritual authority is spiritual edification.

In God's thought, authority and the spirit of the cross go hand in hand. And this principle is exhibited throughout Paul's entire apostolic ministry.

It should be understood that the canonical (Biblical) writings penned by Paul and the other apostles are inspired and authoritative in their own right. They embody God's voice in holy Scripture. In this chapter, however, we have been looking at Paul's writings with an eye to seeing the relationship between a worker and a church. When we look at Paul's letters through this lens, we discover that he was nonauthoritarian.

The Nonauthoritarianism of Other Apostles

Let us look at how other first-century apostles viewed spiritual authority. Timothy was as nonauthoritarian as Paul. Paul never gave his young co-worker license to exert formal power over the saints. He rather encouraged him to "exhort" the saints in meekness. He also instructed him to cultivate a family-like relationship with the church (1 Tim. 5:1-2; 2 Tim. 2:24-25; 4:2).

In one place, Paul instructs him with the words, "these things command (*paraggello*) and teach" (1 Tim. 4:11). But the *things* that Paul exhorts Timothy to "command" are the words of the Spirit (4:1). And they are informed by sound teaching (4:6). Like Paul, Timothy worked *with* not *over* people.

Paul's admonition to Titus is similar. In Titus 2:15, Paul's charge to "teach, exhort, and reprove *these things* with all authority (*epitage*)" is to be understood against the backdrop of his earlier injunction. That injunction was: "But as for you, speak the things which are fitting for sound doctrine" (Titus 2:1). In other words, Titus was free to authoritatively speak, reprove, and exhort those things that mirror the sound teaching of Jesus Christ. (For authority is vested in the latter.)

The letters of John breathe the same nonauthoritarian air. Like Paul, John did not meddle in church affairs. Nor did he claim a right to rule the saints. When Diotrephes was usurping authority in one church, John did not seek to force him out. He rather exhorted the saints not to follow those who do evil (3 John 9-11).

John concedes that he has no commandant to give (1 John 2:7; 2 John 5-6). Instead, he points to Christ's new commandment—which is love. In all these ways, John's outlook on authority is very Pauline.

Again, the inescapable conclusion in all this is that apostolic workers do not have official authority over churches. They do not assume formal possession of them. Nor do they turn them into franchises (or virtual denominations) of their own peculiar ministries.

Apostolic workers, if authentic, use their ministries to serve the churches. They do not use the churches to build their ministries!

The ministry of the first-century apostle, then, was a service rather than an expression of dominance. This is why

Paul referred to the churches he planted in explicitly non-hierarchical terms. He called them "brethren" and "partners" in ministry (2 Cor. 5:20-6:1; 7:3; Phil. 1:5,7; 2:17). When he spoke to them, he spoke as one of their own—as an equal. He did not speak as one who was above or over them (1 Cor. 5:2-3; Col 2:5).

In this way, NT apostles did not control the churches. Neither did the churches control the apostles. Paul's words in Galatians 4:12 capture the thrust of his cooperative and relational mindset: *"Become as I am, for I also have become as you are . . . " (NASB).*

Paul's Confidence in the Churches

Unlike modern clergy, Paul had great confidence in the churches he planted. He was assured that the believing communities would obey God. He was also confident that they would function properly in his absence. Consider the following texts:

I have CONFIDENCE IN YOU IN THE LORD THAT YOU will adopt no other view. (Gal. 5:10, NASB)

WE HAVE CONFIDENCE IN THE LORD THAT YOU are doing and will continue to do the things we command. (2 Thess. 3:4)

I HAD CONFIDENCE IN ALL OF YOU, that you would all share my joy. (2 Cor. 2:3)

I am glad I CAN HAVE COMPLETE CONFIDENCE IN YOU. (2 Cor. 7:16)

In addition, we are sending with them our brother who has often proved to us in many ways that he is zealous, and now even more so because of HIS GREAT CONFIDENCE IN YOU. (2 Cor. 8:22)

I MYSELF AM CONVINCED, MY BROTHERS, THAT YOU yourselves are full of goodness, complete in knowledge and competent to instruct one another. (Rom. 15:14)

CONFIDENT OF YOUR OBEDIENCE, I write to you, knowing that you will do even more than I ask. (Phlm. 21)

BEING CONFIDENT OF THIS, that he who began a good work in you will carry it on to completion until the day of Christ Jesus. (Php. 1:6)

Even though we speak like this, dear friends, WE ARE CONFIDENT OF BETTER THINGS IN YOUR CASE—things that accompany salvation. (Heb. 6:9, author unknown)

Even in the midst of the chaotic meetings at Corinth, Paul never once put a choke-hold on the church's open participatory gatherings. Nor did he prohibit the brethren from exercising their gifts. Rather, he gave them broad guidelines to facilitate the orderliness of their meetings. And he trusted that they would adhere to them (1 Cor. 14:1ff.).

While modern clergy leaders feel they cannot "allow" their fellow brethren (in their congregations) to freely function in their gifts lest they "spin out of control," the path of Paul's thought runs in a radically different direction.

First, Paul did not see himself as having the right to "prohibit" or "allow" God's people to function in the church. No man has that right!

Second, Paul had complete confidence in his ministry. So much so that he trusted the churches to have open participatory meetings without *any* human officiation. Including his own! In this way, Paul built well. He worked toward equipping the saints to function in his absence.

In sharp contradiction, when modern clergy leaders express their lack of confidence in God's people to minister effectively in an open church meeting, they are indicting their own ministries! For nothing so tests the quality of the saints' equipping than to have them minister one to another in an open participatory gathering.

When we look at the Christian landscape from that terrain, it goes without saying that real equipping is never produced by preaching 45-minute sermons every Sunday! Listening to sermons while frozen in pews fosters a muted priesthood. It does not produce spiritual growth. (See *Rethinking the Wineskin* for further details on the first-century church meeting.)

Paul's Relationship with His Co-Workers

Let us shift our attention to Paul's relationship with his co-workers. How did Paul treat those brethren who were part of his apostolic team?

Spiritual authority was expressed within the sphere of apostolic work. And Paul was the center of his apostolic band. (Note that Paul and the other workers were not independent free-lancers. They always moved in association with a circle of co-laborers. This is virtually never the case with today's self-advancing "apostles".)

Paul clearly took responsibility for the direction of the work. He also had no problem administering the movements of his co-workers (Acts 16:1-4,9-10; 17:15; 19:21-22; 20:3-5,13-15; 1 Cor. 4:17; 2 Cor. 8:18-23; Eph. 6:21-22; Phil. 2:19,23,25,28; Col. 4:8-9; 2 Tim. 4:9-13,20-22; Titus 1:5; 3:12-13). Yet a fixed hierarchical system did not work among Paul's company. Paul was not the president or CEO of the work!

For this reason we never see Paul demanding his co-laborers to thoughtless obedience. As with the churches, Paul sought the voluntary consent of his colleagues whenever he made a request of them (1 Cor. 16:10-12; 2 Cor. 8:6,16-18; 9:5; 12:18; Phil. 2:22-23).

At times, Paul subjected himself to the wishes of his fellow workers (1 Cor. 16:12). He also allowed room for them to disagree with him (Acts 15:36-41). The sending of Titus mentioned in 2 Corinthians 8:17 underscores the participatory relationship that Paul had with his co-workers: *"For he [Titus] not only accepted our appeal, but being himself very earnest, he has gone to you of his own accord."*

Paul took the lead in the sphere of his apostolic work simply because he was more spiritually advanced than his co-workers. It was not because he had a higher position in the ecclesiastical pyramid. Cooperation rather than authoritarianism marked Paul's dealings with his co-laborers.

Because Paul exerted spiritual authority in the work, subjection in Paul's circle was voluntary and personal. It was never formal or official. Strikingly, Paul did not regard the original twelve as having some sort of hierarchical authority over him. Nor did he have any regard for "apostolic" status (Gal. 2:6-9). Recall that on one occasion, Paul rebuked one of the most prominent apostles in public when an essential truth was at stake (Gal. 2:11-21).

Apostles are Dependent on the Body

The notion that holds that apostolic workers have ruling authority over local churches is untenable. So is the idea that some workers have official authority over other workers.

These ideas are inventions of natural minds. And they are dissonant with Paul's actual practice.

Apostolic workers, just like all other ministries in the Body of Christ, are dependent upon *the Body* to receive Christ's fullness. This is clear from Paul's opening words to the Romans. There he states that he is eager to not only bless them by his gifts (1:11), but to receive help through theirs (1:12; 15:32).

We do well to remember that independence and individualism are always condemned by God. Dependence upon God never renders us independent of one another. The Lord never permits His people to "do what is right in their own eyes" (Deut. 12:8). For "he who separates himself *seeks his own way* and quarrels against all sound wisdom" (Prov. 18:1).

God, therefore, has not consigned any of us, including workers, into a little cubicle of our own existence where we may choose our own way. Those who conceive of their relationship with the Lord as wholly vertical ("me and Jesus alone") are deceived and fulfill the words of the sage: *"The way of a fool is right in his own eyes, but a wise man is he who listens to counsel" (Prov. 12:15).*

No matter how spiritual a believer may be, he is never exempted from his need for the supply of his brothers and sisters in Christ. For even the mighty Moses needed the help of Aaron and Hur to strengthen his hands in the evil day (Exod. 17:10-13).

Of course, all that has been said is not tantamount to denying that apostolic workers do possess spiritual authority. For they do. But again, spiritual authority is something far different from positional/hierarchal authority.

In the Lord, authority exists. But it is attached to function, not to office. There is a tremendous difference between responding to function and responding to office. Office separates brethren. But Spirit-bestowed function builds them together.

As we have seen, Paul's letters clearly display a non-authoritarian mind at work. They are also saturated with a cooperative tone. Yet because many modern Christians come to the NT with the preconceived idea that apostles have tremendous delegated authority, they miss the non-authoritarian strain that liberally flows from Paul's pen. For this reason, today's popular notion of apostolic authority is unquestionably non-Pauline.

Apostolic Ministry Today

There is no shortage of self-styled, self-appointed, post-Pauline "apostles" running to and fro in the Body of Christ today. Such ones issue authoritarian decrees, claim followers, and build empires. As a result, many discerning Christians have concluded that apostles do not exist anymore.

Let it be known, however, that God *has* raised up genuine apostolic workers in this century. These are those who have walked—and *are walking*—in a Pauline spirit. Like Paul, these workers are not interested in building Christian empires nor in starting movements. Neither do they have any interest in reaching celebrity status (1 Cor. 1:13; 3:7,21).

What, then, does a contemporary apostolic worker look like? If you are part of the institutional church scene, you have probably never seen one. Yes, you have undoubtedly seen those who claim to be apostles. At the very least, you have heard of men who had the word "apostle" wrapped around them by others. Yet such men frequently lack the goods of a genuine worker.

By contrast, true workers are those who *hide* themselves rather than those who *hustle* themselves. Their work is largely unseen. Their service frequently unnoticed. Real workers do not build denominations, programs, missions, buildings, or para-church organizations! They exclusively build the *ekklesia* of Jesus Christ! (Note that God uses the humble in heart to build His house—Isa. 66:1-2.)

What is more, they do not go around announcing that they are apostles! In fact, there is a real good chance they do not even like this term. And since they are not part of the latest spiritual fads, you will not find them belonging to any organized church or movement. Nor will you (normally) find them in the Christian tabloids.

While they are less in number than the extravagant and conspicuous "super-apostles" of our time, true workers are making deeper inroads towards God's eternal purpose in Christ. This is because they are building *His* church in *His* way.

All of this translates into the following simple pre-scription: Modern Christians should be *cognizant* of their need for apostolic ministry, *generous* in their support of apostolic workers, yet *cautious* of those claiming to have apostolic status.

CHAPTER 6

SUMMARY AND CONCLUSION

When our Lord Jesus was on earth, the religious leaders of His day pressed the vexing question: *"By what authority do you do these things, and who gave you this authority?"* (Matt. 21:23).

Ironically, not a few in today's religious establishment are raising the same question to those simple groups who are gathering around Jesus Christ alone—without clerical control or denominational partisanism.

"Who is your covering?" is essentially the same question as, "By what authority do you do these things?"

As I have shown, this question is rooted in a false interpretation of Scripture. At bottom, the modern notion of ecclesiastical "covering" is a thinly veiled euphemism for control. For this reason it maps poorly with God's idea of mutual subjection. And it represents a wholesale departure from NT principle.

While those who take their cues from the institutional church carry on rather loudly about it, "covering" would be repudiated by all first-century Christians. To be sure, ideological divisions, doctrinal heresies, anarchic independence, and individualistic subjectivism are severe problems that plague the Body of Christ today. But denominational/clerical "covering" is bad medicine for purging these ills.

The "covering" teaching is really a symptom of the same problem masquerading as a solution. As such, it compounds the problems of rugged individualism and independence by blurring the distinction between official and organic authority. It creates a false sense of security among believers. And it introduces further divisions in the Body of Christ.

Just as serious, the "covering" teaching inoculates the believing priesthood from carrying out its God-ordained responsibility to function in spiritual matters. Intentional or not, "covering" strikes fear into the hearts of multitudes of Christians. It asserts that if you take responsibility in spiritual things without the approval of an "ordained" clergyman, you will be raw meat for the enemy!

Today's clergy chew up a great deal of Christian air-time touting how necessary they are to your spiritual well-being. They assert that they are essential for providing direction and stability in the church. It is the old "without-a-vision-the-people-perish" sermon. But it is routinely the *clergyman's* isolated vision that you are hopelessly perishing without!

In this way, the covering teaching contains an implicit threat that the "uncovered" are to blame for all the horrible things that will happen to them. Few things so paralyze the ministry of the Body than does the doctrine of "covering."

Consequently, if we try to finesse the ills of the church by employing a technique of "covering," we shall end up with an illness that is worse than the maladies it is intended to cure.

To put it succinctly, the "covering" teaching brings with it very specific tones, textures, and resonances that have little to do with Jesus, Paul, or any other apostle. While it avows to scratch a peculiarly modern itch, it is alien to God's chosen method for displaying His authority.

The spiritual antidote for the ills of heresy, independence, and individualism is not "covering." It is mutual subjection to the Spirit of God and to one another out of reverence for Christ. Nothing short of this can protect the Body of Christ. Nothing less can heal its open wounds.

Mutual Subjection is Natural to the Christian Life

Make no mistake about it. If you are functioning according to God's desire, you will be mutually subject to your fellow brethren with whom you fellowship. You will also gladly receive counsel from those proven brethren who are ahead of you in the Lord.

Properly conceived, mutual subjection is not idealistic. It is practical and vital. It exists when one living stone in the Lord's house humbly receives help from other living stones in a living way. It stems from the sober awareness that because you are connected to your brothers and sisters in Christ, your actions and attitudes profoundly affect theirs.

In this way, mutual subjection creates a culture that appreciates spiritual leadership without absolutizing it. It responds to spiritual authority without turning it into an instrument of control. For when "mentoring relationships" and "accountability partnerships" are governed by mutual subjection, they become spiritually healthy and mutually enriching. They also bear no resemblance to the modern practice of hierarchal "covering."

Personal Testimony

As one who has met with several first-century styled churches since the 1980s, I have experienced the immense benefit of mutual subjection. In particular, I have discovered the safety that comes from bringing crucial matters of my life and ministry before the judgment of the church. I have also experienced the wisdom in waiting for a consensus before moving forward.

In addition, I have been tremendously helped by tested fellow workers in other places with whom I have developed relationships. While there is not the slightest hint of any official or formal relationship among us, I joyfully and unashamedly take counsel from them whenever I am faced with a difficult issue. For I have grown to trust their discernment.

Many times their counsel confirmed what the Lord revealed to me personally. In times when I had a blind spot, God used them to adjust my thinking. Admittedly, if I had not heeded their counsel on these occasions, I would have landed myself into very troubling waters.

By the same token, these brethren have been humble enough to receive help from me. This affirms that spiritual subjection is always *mutual*. Such relationships are wonderfully refreshing. They are naturally spontaneous and incredibly informal. But they are profoundly necessary for maintaining and deepening spiritual development.

Relationships of this sort evoke growth in love for Christ and others. They safeguard us from error. They also strike a delicate balance between the trappings of cliquish separation and a pathological dependence upon others.

When mentoring relationships get deified and devolve into command-styled relationships, they rest on the cusp of idolatry. At the same time, when they are severed or absent, they lead to alienation.

Mutual subjection, then, diverges from those systems that create a context where people end up obsessing on relationships and those that foster an unhealthy isolation from the Body of Christ.

The Crux of the Whole Matter

In closing, I wish to highlight the reason why this discussion of "protective covering" deserves the attention I have given it. It is because it fundamentally suppresses the executive Headship of the Lord Jesus Christ. Bogus interpretations and applications of leadership, authority, and accountability always amount to stifling His Headship in His church.

This explains why this issue is so delicate. The enemy knows that if he can deceive God's people on these points, he can effectively supplant the rightful place of Jesus in the believing community. And this thwarts the full purpose of God. Not to mention the untold damage it does to God's people.

Therefore, the attempt to critically examine the "covering" teaching and all that is bound up with it is far more than an arcane, theological exercise. It touches the very purpose of God. A purpose that is wholly occupied with the absolute sovereignty and supremacy of Jesus Christ.

Mutual subjection helps to underscore the Bible's central motif: The universal preeminence of Christ (Eph. 1:9-10; Col. 1:15-20). For when the church learns to be subject to Jesus in everything, God's eternal purpose of bringing all things into subjective obedience to His Son will be fulfilled (Col. 1:18).

As the "firstfruits of God's creation" (Jas. 1:18), we Christians must first learn to be subject to spiritual authority. As we do, the whole creation will follow suit. This is what makes subjection to Divine authority both precious and serious.

A New Awakening

I sincerely hope that what you have read in this book will help to dismantle the sectarian barriers that stem from the modern "covering" teaching. At the very least, I trust that you will be provoked to rethink your notion of leadership and authority.

If you have properly understood and received my message, the following will happen: You will realize that you run grave spiritual risks by acting condemnatory and smug toward those churches and ministries that have chosen not to wed themselves to a denomination or a religious institution. You will cease from uttering "no covering" platitudes and thoughtlessly waving your hands at buzz words like "accountability."

Equally so, you will learn to recognize the Lord's anointing upon the most simple fellowships—no longer writing them off because they do not fit modern self-constructed leadership styles. You will also exercise a bit more care when judging the legitimacy of a church or ministry. Finally, you will cease from making blanket statements about "covering" and "accountability"—statements that are based upon misappropriations of the NT.

In the 1970s, God raised up many NT-styled house churches in virtually every part of America. Yet misteaching about spiritual authority caused the demise of virtually all of them. Tragically, they experienced the "smothering" that follows "covering!"

May it not be so in our day.

While we are subject to the same foibles as those who have gone before us, we do not have to succumb to their mistakes. If we have to make mistakes, let us make new ones!

As in the 1970s, the Lord is now re-awakening His people to His all-consuming purpose of restoring His house. In the light of this awakening, may you receive the new wine of His Spirit (which is Jesus Christ). And may you scrap the old leaking wineskins that have hindered His flow.

Would to God that there would be scores of Christian groups who are gathering unto His Son *alone*. Groups that express His Body in all of its fullness. Groups that are not hidebound by authoritarian leadership models or denominational structures.

May you, dear reader, be added to their number!

Perhaps a closing metaphor will help sum up all I have said in the foregoing pages. We can compare mutual subjection to good music. When mutual subjection functions in the context of intelligent humility and deep faithfulness to the Headship of Christ, it makes a beautiful melody that resonates with the sweet harmony of the NT song. But when it is replaced by hierarchical systems that characterize the spirit of the Gentiles, its sound is distorted and damaging. Still worse, when it is rejected in favor of the postmodern sins of wholesale individualism and independence, its timbre and key ceases altogether. And the dead chill of silence stands in its wake.

BIBLIOGRAPHY

The following annotated bibliography contains further reading material germane to the subjects dealt with in this book. (See also the bibliography in *Rethinking the Wineskin*.)

Allen, Roland. *Missionary Methods: St. Paul's or Ours?*, Eerdmans. An excellent treatment of the Pauline method of church planting. Allen was far ahead of his time.

Banks, Robert. "Church Order and Government," *Dictionary of Paul and His Letters: A Compendium of Contemporary Biblical Scholarship*. Excellent, fact-laden discussion of the Pauline concept of authority, church order, and apostolic work.

_____. *Paul's Idea of Community*, Hendrickson. One of the most theologically substantial books available on Paul's view of authority, leadership, and apostolic work written by a first-rate NT scholar.

Barrs, Jerram. *Shepherds and Sheep: A Biblical View of Leading and Following*, InterVarsity Press. Decent critique of the "discipleship/shepherding movement" of the 1970s. While I disagree with Barrs' contention that apostles are no longer extant in the church, the book is valuable nonetheless.

Best, Ernest. *Paul and His Converts*, T. & T. Clark. Scholarly look at how Paul related to the churches that he founded.

Bryson, George. "Excuse for Abuse: An Examination of Heavy-Handed Authority Doctrines," *The Word for Today*. Good discussion about the problem of spiritual abuse in the church.

Burks, Ron and Viki. *Damaged Disciples: Casualties of Authoritarian Churches and the Shepherding Movement*, Zondervan. Helpful look at the "discipleship/shepherding movement" through the eyes of two former participants.

Campbell, R.A. *The Elders: Seniority in Earliest Christianity*, T. & T. Clark. The most recent and most thorough examination of eldership among the first-century Jews and Christians.

Campenhausen, Hans Von. *Ecclesiastical Authority and Spiritual Power in the Church of the First Three Centuries*, Stanford University Press. Although some of its conclusions are flawed, this work contains many valuable insights into the subjects of church authority and ecclesiastical power from a historical perspective.

Coleman, Steve. "A Christian Look at the Shepherding Movement," *Personal Freedom Outreach*, 3:2. Helpful discussion of this movement.

Dunn, James D.G. *New Testament Theology in Dialogue*, Westminister Press. Contains an outstanding discussion about the error of the "clergy/laity" system and the modern idea of ordination. Dunn is one of today's foremost NT scholars.

Edwards, Gene. *A Tale of Three Kings*, Tyndale. This book discusses the problem of authoritarian abuse by drawing instructional imagery from King David's life. While it focuses on how God can effect brokenness in a person's life through authoritarian personalities, the book has been employed by some leaders as a justification for clerical control.

_____.*Letters to a Devastated Christian*, SeedSowers. A series of personal letters designed to help heal disillusioned Christians who have been bruised and embittered by authoritarian groups.

_____. *Rethinking Elders*, SeedSowers. Unique study of elders from the NT story.

_____. *Revolution: The Story of the Early Church*, SeedSowers. Excellent overview describing how the early church was built through apostolic ministry.

Enroth, Ronald. *Churches That Abuse*, Zondervan. Deals with authoritarian churches and their effect on Christians.

Holmberg, Brengt. *Paul and Power: The Structure of Authority in the Primitive Church as Reflected in the Pauline Epistles*, Fortress Press. Scholarly look at Paul's idea of power and authority.

Ketcherside, W. Carl. *The Twisted Scriptures*, Diversity Press. Insightfully candid discussion about the perils of factionalism and partisanism in the church.

Lang, G.H. *The Churches of God*, Schoettle Publishing. This work contains some helpful chapters on modern denominationalism as well as Biblical decision-making in the church. Available from the publisher at P.O. Box 1246, Hayesville, NC 28904.

Miller, Hal. "Leadership in the Church: Ten Propositions," *Searching Together*, Vol. 1, No. 3, Word of Life Church. One of the best essays on NT leadership available.

_____. "Nuts and Bolts of Authority and Leadership," *Voices Newsletter*, No. 4. Practical and thought-provoking exposition of the essence of NT leadership and authority.

Miller, Marlin. "The Recasting of Authority." *Sojourners* (February 1979). Superb discussion of the NT concept of leadership and authority.

Miller, Paul. *Leading the Family of God*, Herald Press. Contains an excellent and practical discussion of how decision-making is to be made in the church.

Nee, Watchman. *The Normal Christian Church Life*, Living Stream Ministry. Seminal classic on the NT church and genuine apostolic work. It thoroughly explores the nature of the apostle's ministry as well as the problem of modern denominationalism. Its only weakness lies in Nee's usage of "official" language. But while Nee makes occasional use of non-Biblical labels, his understanding of authority is predominantly functional.

_____. *Spiritual Authority*, Christian Fellowship Publishers. One of the most abused pieces of literature ever to be written in this century.

Virtually every recent authoritarian movement has gotten mileage out of this book to support the power of heavy-handed leadership. While the book does contain some precious insights, its weaknesses render it dangerous in the wrong hands. Regrettably, Nee's book blurs the distinction between the Old and New Testament concept of authority and fails to distinguish between the way it works among dignitaries versus the church. In Nee's defense, this book was never intended for a general audience. It is merely a transcription of messages that he gave to his apostolic co-workers in China.

Quebedeaux, Richard. *By What Authority: The Rise of Personality Cults in American Christianity*, Harper & Row. Insightful look at the problem of personality cultism and the abuse of authority.

Schütz, J.H. *Paul and the Anatomy of Apostolic Authority*, Cambridge University Press. Careful analysis of Paul's view of apostolic authority.

Smith, Christian. "Church Without Clergy," *Voices in the Wilderness*, (Nov/Dec 1988). Penetrating discussion of the practical peril of the "clergy/laity" schema.

_____. *Going to the Root*, Herald Press. Contains several terrific chapters on leadership, accountability, and decision-making in the church.

Stabbert, Bruce. *The Team Concept*, Hegg Brothers Printing. Thorough discussion of the NT teaching on elders.

Viola, Frank. *Rethinking the Wineskin: The Practice of the New Testament Church (Third Edition)*, Present Testimony Ministry. This book sets forth the basis for the book you hold in your hands.

_____. *So You Want to Start a House Church?*, Present Testimony Ministry. This book discusses how apostolic workers planted churches in the first century and how they still do today. Available at www.ptmin.org

_____. *Straight Talk to Elders*, Present Testimony Ministry. Comprehensive study of elders from the NT and church history. Available at www.ptmin.org

_____, at el. *The House Church Movement: Which Direction Will It Take?* SeedSowers. Discusses how NT-styled churches are led today.

White, John and Blue, Ken. *Healing the Wounded: The Costly Love of Church Discipline*, InterVarsity Press. Helpful study on the Biblical concept of church discipline. Includes John H. Yoder's article, "Binding and Loosing" in the appendix.

Yoder, Howard. "Binding and Loosing," *Concern*, No. 14 (February, 1967). Insightful discussion of NT-styled church discipline.

_____. "The Fullness of Christ, Perspectives on Ministries in Renewal." *Concern*, No. 17 (February, 1969). A masterful and sophisticated portrayal of the NT concept of leadership and authority.

Zens, Jon. "Building Up the Body: One Man or One Another?," *Searching Together*, Vol. 10, No. 2, Word of Life Church. Superb treatment on how the Body of Christ is called to function in ministry. (See also ST editions 11:3; 13:1; 13:3; 21:1-4; 23:4.)

OTHER BOOKS IN THIS SERIES

Volume 1: Rethinking the Wineskin: The Practice of the New Testament Church (Revised Third Edition). This is Frank Viola's classic book on the first-century church. It demonstrates beyond dispute that the modern institutional church has no Scriptural right to exist!

Volume 3: Pagan Christianity: The Origins of Our Modern Church Practices. A unique work that traces every modern Protestant practice, proving that it has no root in the NT.

Volume 4: So You Want to Start a House Church? First-Century Styled Church Planting. A must read after completing *Rethinking the Wineskin*. This book discusses the apostolic pattern for planting NT-styled churches. It also answers the question: "What shall I do now that I have left the organized church?"

Volume 5: From Nazareth to Patmos: The Saga of the New Testament Church. A synopsis of the entire story of the first-century church that traces the Kingdom of God in chronological order.

Straight Talk to Elders. This book could have just as easily been titled *Straight Talk to Pastors*. A thorough survey from Matthew to Revelation on the role and function of first-century elders (pastors).

Knowing Christ Together. An insightful book that explores the subject of knowing and walking with the Lord with other believers.

The Untold Story of the New Testament Church: An Extraordinary Guide to Understanding the New Testament. A detailed re-telling of the entire story of the first-century church in chronological order.

For these titles and more, visit our ever-growing web site. It is full of resources, free articles, and on-line messages about Christ and His church. Go to: **www.ptmin.org**

To obtain further information about first-century styled church life, email us at **PTMIN@aol.com**